MY RECIPES
CASA GUSTO

Pascal
BOSCH

MY RECIPES
CASA GUSTO

Pascal
BOSCH

CULINART

Édition : BoD · Books on Demand GmbH, In de Tarpen 42,

22848 Norderstedt (Allemagne)

Impression : Libri Plureos GmbH, Friedensallee 273,

22763 Hamburg (Allemagne)

Illustration: Casa Gsuto

ISBN : 978-2-3225-4272-7

Dépôt légal : Novembre 2024

My Recipes... For You!

Since opening my restaurant six years ago, I have had the pleasure of meeting and serving over 16,000 customers. Every day, as I greet my guests, I receive numerous requests to share my recipes and culinary secrets.

It is always a great pleasure to see the enthusiasm and curiosity of my customers for the cuisine I prepare with passion.

I have decided to take the plunge and am delighted to present to you my book, born from these warm exchanges and the desire to share with you the recipes that have made my restaurant a success. Inside, you will find dishes that have delighted your taste buds and tips to recreate them at home.

I would like to thank each and every one of you for your loyalty and support. Without you, this culinary adventure would not have been possible. Thank you for being part of this beautiful story.

Bon appétit and happy cooking!

Pascal

Table des matières

My Meats

My Fish

Around the Aperitif

My Sangria

For 1 liter of sangria, you will need:

- 55 cl of red wine
- 35 cl of apple juice
- 10 cl of Liqueur 43
- 2 tablespoons of powdered sugar
- 1 apple, 1 orange, and 1 Canarian banana

Mix the ingredients and let it rest for a few hours in the refrigerator before enjoying it well chilled.

Chorizo Puff Pastry

Here is an easy recipe that will impress your guests.

You will need:

- Puff pastry
- 150 g of chorizo
- 100 g of grated Gruyère cheese
- 1 tablespoon of crème fraîche
- 1 egg

In a blender, finely chop the chorizo with the egg and crème fraîche.

Transfer to a mixing bowl and add the grated Gruyère cheese. Mix everything until you get a homogeneous paste.

On your work surface, roll out your puff pastry.

Spread your chorizo mixture evenly over the entire surface of the pastry.

Roll the pastry to form a log about 4 cm in diameter and refrigerate it for 1 hour to harden.

After this time, you can now cut your slices about 1 cm thick. Place them on your baking sheet.

Using a brush, glaze your chorizo slices with an egg yolk diluted in water.

You can now place your baking sheet in the oven, which you have preheated to 180°C.

Remove from the oven when the slices are golden brown. Ten minutes should be enough.

Enjoy warm!

In your base preparation, you can add chopped parsley, coriander, and/or any spices to your taste.

For convenience, I prefer square or rectangular puff pastry rather than round.

To prevent the puff pastry from sticking during baking, do not hesitate to place a parchment paper sheet on your baking sheet.

Homemade Mojo Olives

Start by making your base sauce by chopping 50 g of basil leaves and 1 garlic clove.

Add 1 teaspoon of five-peppercorn blend and a pinch of salt. Quickly emulsify with 10 cl of olive oil.

Add 1 teaspoon of piri-piri, 1 teaspoon of Herbes de Provence, and 1 tablespoon of powdered sugar.

You can now marinate your olives. It's best to prepare them in the morning to serve them in the evening. This way, they will have time to absorb all the flavors.

I prefer olives stuffed with anchovies. In this case, be careful with the salt!

You can add a bit of zest to your preparation by adding some lemon zest.

Anchovy Dip

Ingredients:

- 25 anchovy fillets in oil
- 10 cl extra virgin olive oil
- 1 tablespoon capers
- 1 garlic clove
- Pepper

Cut the anchovies into pieces and place them in a mortar with the chopped garlic and capers.

Using a pestle, crush everything with circular motions against the sides of the mortar.

Gradually add the olive oil in a thin stream until you obtain a creamy paste. Pepper to taste.

Serve on toasted baguette slices.

Country Pâté Toasts

During the summer of 2023, I had the idea to offer my clients country pâté toasts to accompany their aperitifs. Given the success, I now offer this pâté for takeaway when I make it. Here is my recipe for 4 people.

- 400 g pork shoulder
- 150 g bacon
- 100 g pork liver
- 1 onion
- 1 shallot
- 2 eggs
- 3 garlic cloves
- 2 tablespoons cognac
- 7 g salt
- 3 g five-peppercorn blend
- 1 tablespoon Piment d'Espelette
- 4 or 5 bay leaves

Chop the meat, bacon, and pork liver. Place the mixture in a mixing bowl.

Finely chop the onion, shallot, and garlic and add them to the meat.

Add the salt, pepper, Piment d'Espelette, cognac, and eggs. Mix everything thoroughly to obtain a homogeneous preparation.

Place the mixing bowl with the preparation in the refrigerator for 12 hours.

Finally, put the preparation into terrines or molds. Personally, I use silicone molds of 14 x 7 cm.

Place the bay leaves on top.

Cook in a bain-marie in an oven at 180°C. The cooking time will depend on the size of your molds.

Let cool for 24 hours.

✋ *To check if your pâté is cooked, insert a knife blade into it. If it comes out dry and clean, it is ready.*

To better preserve them and depending on the container you used, you can place a layer of pork fat on top to extend the shelf life.

I serve this pâté on slices of sandwich bread.

Figs Wrapped in Serrano

Peel 12 figs and cut them in half.

Cut 12 slices of Serrano ham in half lengthwise.

Wrap each fig piece in a slice of Serrano ham. Secure with a toothpick.

Place everything on a plate and drizzle a few drops of white Martini before serving at room temperature.

Agua de Valencia

This isn't my creation, but it's so delicious that I can't help but share the recipe with you.

Ingredients for 4 people:

- 330 ml fresh orange juice
- 160 ml Gin
- 160 ml Vodka
- 330 ml Cava
- A few ice cubes

In a pitcher, pour the orange juice, add the gin and vodka.

Finally, add the cava.

Stir gently and refrigerate for an hour. Serve with a few ice cubes and orange slices.

My Starters

Provencal Stewed Mussels

For 2 people, you will need:

- 24 to 30 mussels, depending on their size and your appetite
- 250 g crushed tomatoes
- ¼ red bell pepper
- ¼ yellow bell pepper
- ½ carrot
- ½ onion
- 2 garlic cloves
- 15 cl white wine
- 20 g smoked bacon
- 1 Paris mushroom
- 1 teaspoon powdered sugar
- 2 teaspoons Herbes de Provence
- 15 cl vegetable broth
- Salt and crushed pepper
- 5 cl olive oil

Clean the mussels and set them aside.

Finely chop the garlic, onion, carrot, and bell peppers.

In a saucepan, sauté everything in olive oil until golden.

Pour in the white wine and let it reduce for 2 minutes over medium heat. Then add the vegetable broth and bring it back to a boil.

Add the tomatoes, mussels, sugar, and Herbes de Provence. Season with salt and pepper. Cook over medium heat until the mussels open.

Taste and adjust the seasoning if necessary.

Finally, add the bacon and the mushroom cut into quarters, stir, and let simmer for another 2 minutes.

Serve hot in a soup plate or a small pot.

Sprinkle with chopped parsley.

You can serve your mussels with a green salad and some toasted bread.

Baked Camembert, Pears Cooked in Red Wine, and Tomato Basil Marmalade

Recipe in 3 steps

I – Pears in Red Wine

Peel 3 pears, remove the core, and cut them lengthwise into 4 or 6 pieces, depending on their size.

Using a zester, take the zest of one lemon.

In a saucepan, pour ½ liter of good quality red wine, 70g of powdered sugar, ½ vanilla pod split in half, and a pinch of cinnamon.

Add the pears and cook over low heat for 30 minutes.

Remove and let cool.

II - Tomato Marmalade

Remove the stem of 500 g of ripe tomatoes with a knife. To make peeling easier, make a cross-shaped incision on the opposite side of the tomatoes.

Dip the tomatoes in boiling water for about 8 seconds and immediately plunge them into a bowl of ice water.

Wait a few seconds, and you will see that you can easily remove the skin from the tomatoes.

In cooking, this action is called "blanching tomatoes."

Now, you can cut your tomatoes into pieces. Put them in a saucepan.

Add 200 g of sugar, a small pinch of salt, and the juice of ½ lemon.

Cook over low heat for an hour, stirring occasionally.

Blend your preparation to obtain a nice texture and place it back on low heat for 45 minutes.

Transfer the marmalade to a container at your desired consistency. Add 1 generous tablespoon of dried basil. Let cool.

✋ *Ideally, cook in a copper container, stainless steel as a default.*

III - Camembert and Plating

In an oven-safe dish, place 3 slices of baguette lightly brushed with olive oil.

Cut ¼ of a Camembert into three equal parts and place them on each toast. Lightly pepper and finish by adding a few drops of olive oil.

Place the dish in your oven at 180°C for 6 to 7 minutes.

On a plate, place 3 pieces of pear.

Take out your Camembert toasts and place them on top of the pears.

Over everything, scatter a few teaspoons of your tomato basil marmalade.

✋ *The pears will release their flavors if served at room temperature.*

Finish by decorating your plate with, for example, one or two fresh basil leaves.

Andalusian-Style Gazpacho with White Fish and Goat Cheese Honey Ice Cream

Recipe in three steps

I – The Ice Cream

You will need:

- 50 g fresh goat cheese
- 250 ml heavy cream
- 15 cl milk
- 2 large egg yolks
- 1 tablespoon powdered sugar
- 2 generous tablespoons honey

In a saucepan, heat the cream and milk over low heat. In a mixing bowl, whisk the egg yolks and sugar until pale.

When the milk and cream start to simmer, pour a small amount over the eggs and sugar. Mix vigorously.

Pour this mixture back into the saucepan, whisk, and cook over low heat until thickened.

Now you can incorporate the liquid honey and small pieces of goat cheese. Whisk again until you obtain a homogeneous mixture.

Place the ice cream in an ice cream maker for 25 minutes.

Transfer to a container and place your beautiful ice cream in the freezer.

II - The Gaspacho (for 2 people)

Ingredients:

- 250 g ripe tomatoes
- 80 g cucumber
- 80 g green bell pepper
- 80 g onion
- 1 small garlic clove
- 3 cl olive oil
- 2 cl Xérès vinegar
- 50 g sandwich bread
- Salt and pepper

Blanch the tomatoes and remove as many seeds as possible. Do the same for the bell pepper.

Cut everything into quarters and place them in a mixing bowl.

Add the cucumber, minced garlic, and onion.

Add the olive oil, salt, and pepper and stir.

Cover the bowl with plastic wrap and refrigerate for 4 hours to allow all the flavors to meld together.

Cut the sandwich bread into large cubes and place them in a second mixing bowl.

Pour the sherry vinegar over the bread until it is fully absorbed.

Put both preparations in your blender and blend until you obtain a beautiful mixture.

Refrigerate.

✋ *If you want a lighter gazpacho, you can strain it to remove the larger pieces.*

III – The Fish Ceviche (for 2 people)

Cut a nice fillet of white fish (100 to 150 g) into pieces and place it in a mixing bowl. Add 1 tablespoon minced red onion, 1 small tablespoon finely minced red bell pepper, and 2 or 3 drops of piri-piri. Season with salt and pepper and mix gently.

Finally, add enough lemon juice to cover the fish.

After 10 minutes, drain and refrigerate.

✋ *Choose your fish according to your taste. You can opt for cod, pollock, sea bass, scallops, hake, ling, swordfish, sardines, mackerel, red mullet, monkfish, or cod.*
Personally, I prefer firm and tender fish like hake, monkfish, or sea bass.

You can make this recipe with either yellow or green lemon.

To add some freshness to your ceviche, you can incorporate 2 or 3 minced coriander leaves.

For a spicier taste, choose Tabasco®.

IV - Plating

In a soup plate:

Gently place the fish, ensuring there is not too much liquid (lemon juice).

Pour the gazpacho over the fish.

In the center of the plate, gently place a ½ scoop of your ice cream.

Finish by sprinkling your gazpacho with fresh chopped parsley, a few small croutons, a pinch of minced red onion, and some lemon zest.

Duck Foie Gras Marinated with Carlos I Brandy and Lanzarote Salt

You will need:

- 500 g raw foie gras
- 2 tablespoons Carlos I Brandy
- 8 g salt
- 2 g pepper
- 1 teaspoon powdered sugar

Take the foie gras out of the refrigerator in advance to let it rest at room temperature for at least 30 minutes.

When it reaches room temperature, separate the two lobes of the foie gras and remove the bile (greenish traces).

Using a sharp knife, expose the main vein by gently pulling it out with your fingers. Carefully remove the adjacent small veins without cutting the flesh.

Evenly sprinkle the foie gras with salt, pepper, sugar, and Brandy.

Let the foie gras marinate for 2 hours at room temperature.

Next, place one whole lobe at the bottom of a terrine, then layer the other pieces on top. Finish by placing the last lobe on top.

Place the terrine in a dish and add water to create a bain-marie.

When your oven, preheated to 100°C, reaches the temperature, place your preparation in it, covered (with a lid or aluminum foil).

After thirty minutes, take out the terrine and press it down (using any weight) but make sure it is uniform across the surface. This pressing will bring the fat to the top.

Place everything in the refrigerator for at least 12 hours.

Remove the press and collect the solidified fat. Melt it, strain it, and pour it over the foie gras.

You can accompany your foie gras with onion chutney, toasted bread, and a pinch of salt.

Your foie gras will have an optimal taste and release its flavors after 3 days of storage.

If you have the opportunity to vacuum seal it, it can be kept for a few weeks.

***Be aware that according to regulations**, a foie gras must weigh at least 300 grams. The weight of a good foie gras varies between 450 and 600 grams.*

Scallop Carpaccio on a Bed of Cauliflower with Lime Syrup, Extra Virgin Olive Oil "Oleo Teide" from Tenerife, and Fresh Cheese with Saffron

Prepare 125 g of fresh cheese by adding 14 g of saffron powder. Mix with a fork in a mixing bowl and refrigerate.

Prepare the cauliflower.

Remove the leaves and cut the florets with a knife. Wash them.

Blanch them in salted water, drain, and let cool.

Using a slicer, cut them thinly and add a drizzle of olive oil, finely chopped red onions, chopped sun-dried tomatoes, salt, pepper, a hint of chili, a few drops of Xérès vinegar and chopped fresh parsley.

In a ring mold placed on a plate, place a bed of 2 tablespoons of your cauliflower.

Cut your scallops into three or four slices and arrange them in a rosette shape on the cauliflower.

 Drizzle with lime syrup and a few drops of olive oil. Place the fresh cheese around the arrangement using a piping bag fitted with a star tip.
Serve at room temperature.

 Instead of parsley, try fresh coriander.

You can accompany this dish with toasted baguette slices.

Sautéed Shrimp with Mushrooms and Garlic, Flambéed with Pastis

Place your peeled shrimp in a pan (6 to 8 depending on their size and your appetite).

Add 1 tablespoon of olive oil.

Sauté over medium heat for 3 minutes, then add 1 chopped Paris mushroom and 2 sliced garlic cloves.

Cook for an additional minute and flambé with 5 cl of Pastis.

Serve in a hot small pot or a deep plate. Place a slice of lemon on top and sprinkle with chopped fresh parsley.

Oysters Florentine

For 4 servings, you will need:

- 16 oysters
- 150 g of fresh spinach
- 1 dl of fresh cream
- 30 g of grated Gruyère cheese
- Black pepper

Open the oysters, taking care to remove any remaining shell fragments.

Detach the flesh and set it aside.

Arrange the oyster shells in an ovenproof dish.

Distribute the spinach in the shells, then season with salt and pepper.

Place the oysters on top of the spinach and pour the fresh cream over them.

Sprinkle each oyster with grated Gruyère cheese.

Grill in the oven for 3 minutes and serve immediately.

Chorizo Two Ways Cooked in Red Wine Sauce with Onions and Peppers

Prepare your fresh chorizos (3 per person) about 3 to 4 cm long.

Sear them in a pan without any fat. Set them aside.

Cut about ten slices of dry chorizo and set them aside as well.

Prepare your red wine sauce:

- 50 cl of red wine
- ½ onion
- ¼ red bell pepper
- 1 teaspoon of Herbes de Provence
- 1 clove of garlic
- 40 g of butter
- A pinch of salt
- A pinch of crushed pepper
- 20 cl of veal stock
- Chopped parsley

Peel and finely chop the garlic.

Slice the onion and bell pepper.

Sweat everything in a saucepan with the pepper, salt, and butter.

Add the red wine and bring to a boil. You can now add the veal stock and Herbes de Provence.

Let it reduce until you obtain a syrupy texture.

You can now place your chorizos in the sauce and bring everything to a gentle boil.

Serve in a deep plate or a small pot, sprinkle with fresh parsley, and enjoy hot.

You can intensify your sauce by adding a piece of dark chocolate.

If the sauce is a bit too bitter for your taste, add a teaspoon of powdered sugar.

Generally, choose a good quality and characterful wine.

Add 4 to 5 drops of piri-piri if you want to spice up your dish.

Tuna Rillettes on Brioche Toasts

Prepare your rillettes by mixing 125 g of flaked tuna in olive oil, ½ finely chopped red onion, 5 or 6 chive stems, 1 generous tablespoon of chopped parsley, a pinch of salt, and pepper.

Pour this mixture into a blender and finely chop, being careful not to turn it into a puree!

Transfer everything to a mixing bowl and add 125 g of fresh cheese (Saint Môret or Philadelphia).

Mix gently until you obtain a perfectly homogeneous rillette.

Add lemon juice until your rillettes reach a nice consistency.

Cover with plastic wrap and set aside.

Prepare your brioche bread by removing the crusty edges. Toast them in the oven.

Once the toasts have cooled, place them on a dish.

Put your rillettes in a piping bag with a fluted nozzle and pipe the mixture onto each toast (covering the entire surface and about 2.5 cm high).

Top with a peeled and cooked shrimp in olive oil.

Sprinkle with fresh parsley and perhaps a bit of lettuce to add freshness to your dish.

 The correct term for chive stems is "leaves."

If you enjoy a bit of a kick, add a few drops of chili to your rillettes.

Lemon can sometimes be too acidic. If that's the case, feel free to add a teaspoon of powdered sugar to the rillettes.

Tarragon Shrimp Cocktail

For 4 people:

Cook 450 g of unpeeled shrimp in olive oil. Lightly salt and pepper. The cooking time is about 3 minutes, turning them gently to avoid breaking them.

When they are cooked, refrigerate.

Prepare your cocktail sauce (see recipe below).

Once the shrimp are well chilled, peel them and place them in a mixing bowl. Gradually add the cocktail sauce. Not too much, not too little!

In glasses (Margarita, Martini, or Champagne coupe), place a bit of freshly chopped lettuce. Drizzle a few drops of olive oil on top.

Now gently place your shrimp mixture (about 100 g per person).

Top with 1 small tablespoon of cocktail sauce.

Garnish and decorate with lemon slices / lemon zest / fresh chopped parsley / chopped chives / half a cherry tomato.

Vanilla Scallop Tartare

For 4 servings:

- 300 g of fresh scallops
- 1 vanilla bean
- 1 lime
- 2 tablespoons of olive oil
- Salt and pepper

Split the vanilla bean in half and scrape out the seeds with the tip of a knife.

In a mixing bowl, combine the vanilla seeds with the olive oil and lime juice.

Cut the scallops into small cubes.

Add the scallop cubes to the mixing bowl with the vanilla oil. Season with salt and pepper to taste.

Cover the bowl and let it marinate in the refrigerator for about 30 minutes.

Serve the tartare in small bowls.

Octopus Salad, Ray of Sunshine

Thinly slice 400 g of octopus and place it in a pot of cold water. Add salt.

Bring to a gentle boil for 30 minutes. Drain.

Chop ½ red bell pepper, 1 onion, and 1 garlic clove. Chop ½ bunch of parsley.

In a pan, heat 3 tablespoons of olive oil and sauté the onion, bell pepper, and garlic for about 5 minutes over low heat.

Pour 10 cl of dry white wine into this mixture. Cook until partially dry. Add the remaining olive oil and the juice of ½ lemon.

Add the chopped parsley. Season with salt and pepper to taste.

Refrigerate for 2 hours before serving.

Consider adding Espelette pepper to give your recipe a kick.

Mussels Gratin with Saffron and French Emmental

For 2 people:

Clean about 400 g of mussels. Steam them, remove the shells, and set aside.

Cook fine rice vermicelli (angel hair pasta).

Prepare your saffron sauce:

In a saucepan, place ½ finely chopped shallot and sauté in olive oil until golden. Deglaze with white wine and add 5 cl of white wine. Add 7 g of saffron powder. Let simmer for 4 to 5 minutes.

Add 1 glass of fresh cream, chopped sun-dried tomatoes, and fresh parsley.

Season with salt and pepper to taste and let reduce over low heat, whisking until you obtain a creamy consistency.

Add the mussels to this cream and mix gently to avoid damaging them.

Arrange your small ceramic casseroles.

Start by placing a bed of angel hair pasta. Then add the mussels in saffron cream.

Generously top with grated Emmental cheese.

Bake in the oven for about ten minutes until you get a beautiful golden and crispy gratin.

✋ *Try another cheese with more character like Reblochon, Cantal, Saint-Nectaire, or Comté. Be careful with Roquefort, which may not pair well with saffron.*

One day, a customer pointed out that my menu was incorrect because Emmental is Swiss. Here's the truth:

> *Emmentaler, or Emmental, is a hard cheese of Swiss origin, named after the Emme Valley (Emmental in German), a region in the east of the canton of Bern. The name Emmental is also given to similar cheeses, industrial or labeled, produced in other countries, such as French Emmental or German Emmentaler. It is a cooked pressed cheese made from cow's milk. The wheel of Emmentaler AOP has an average weight of 90 kg. The large size of the wheels was due to fiscal reasons: in the 19th century, customs duties were levied on the number of pieces exported, not on their weight.*

> *Emmentaler AOP "traditional aging" undergoes a seven-week aging process, four of which are without film. Its optimal tasting period extends from May to October after a minimum aging of three months, with the period from November to April being slightly less optimal. For a stronger taste, the aging period can extend from 8 to 12 months or even longer. Emmentaler is one of the most consumed cheeses in Switzerland, along with Gruyère. It is the most consumed cheese in*

France, ahead of Camembert. It is also one of the most well-known and exported cheeses in the world.

Production
The production area includes the cantons of Bern, Aargau, Glarus, Lucerne, Schwyz, Solothurn, St. Gallen, Thurgau, Zug, Zurich, and the districts of Lac and Singine in the canton of Fribourg. Emmental AOP is made according to very precise specifications and sold at a price that makes it difficult to produce in small dairies. Thus, while the country had 800 producers in 1990, there were only 149 companies producing Emmental AOC in 2012.

For the first time in 2010, the production of Gruyère AOC (26,300 tons) surpassed the production of Emmental AOC (23,480 tons). Nevertheless, Emmental AOC remains the most exported Swiss cheese with 20,000 tons per year, double that of Gruyère AOC. An industrial cheese is also produced today under the generic name Emmental, in Germany, Austria, Denmark, the United States, France, Finland, Ireland, and the Netherlands. The total European industrial production is around 464,200 tons, representing about 6% of the milk collection in these countries. Currently, and since 1999, France is recognized as the world's leading producer of this cheese, with about 110,000 tons per year (Brittany accounts for about half of this production).

Distribution in France

Detailed articles: Central French Emmental and Emmental de Savoie. Emmental is the most consumed cheese in France with 146,000 tons per year, ahead of Camembert (52,500 tons) and Coulommiers (39,500 tons) (2022 figures). For a long time, the production of industrial French Emmental was distributed in France under the generic name "Gruyère"; the ambiguity arose from the fact that, like Emmental, French Gruyère has holes, unlike Swiss Gruyère which does not. In the mid-19th century, Bernese Emmental merchants entered the French market by passing their product off as Gruyère. This is where the confusion between Gruyère and Emmental originated. Although Emmental is claimed to be a French cheese, the international Stresa convention does not recognize any French origin. As for Gruyère, sold under the IGP Gruyère de France, its wheels are much smaller (about 40 kg), as well as its holes (diameter varying between a pea and a cherry); its texture is more melting and its taste more pronounced than Emmental.

French Emmental is made from French milk, raw or pasteurized. The Label Rouge guarantees production from raw milk, from cows in eastern and central France, fed on grass and hay, and aged for at least 12 weeks. The salt content can be high in some non-organic products; in 2021, it varied between 0.4 and 1 g per 100 g.

The original production is claimed by Switzerland, which obtained an AOC in 2008, as for raclette and Gruyère.

Source: Wikipédia

Roasted Camembert on Toast with Hibiscus Syrup and Saffron Poached Pears

I – Prepare the Hibiscus Flowers

In a bowl filled with cold water, rehydrate a handful of hibiscus flowers overnight.

The next day, place them in a saucepan with half of the water and 3 tablespoons of powdered sugar. Cook and reduce over low heat until you obtain a syrupy consistency.

II – Cook the Pears

Peel 3 pears, remove the core, and cut them lengthwise into 4 or 6 pieces, depending on their size.

Using a zester, take the zest of one lemon.

In a saucepan, pour ½ liter of water, 70g of powdered sugar, ½ split vanilla bean, and a pinch of cinnamon.

Add the pears and cook over low heat for 30 minutes.

Drain and sprinkle 7g of powdered saffron on top.

Mix gently to avoid damaging the pears, then set aside and let cool.

II – The Rest is Child's Play

On a slice of baguette, drizzle a few drops of good quality olive oil.

Place a piece of Camembert on top, then drizzle again with olive oil. Season with crushed five-pepper blend.

Adjust the number of toasts to your appetite and that of your guests, and bake for 10 minutes, until the Camembert starts to melt and turns golden.

On a plate, arrange your saffron poached pear quarters, then place the cheese toasts over the fruits. Finally, sprinkle the hibiscus flowers harmoniously over your appetizer.

Finish with a pinch of freshly chopped parsley.

Fish and Seafood Terrine

You will need:

- 6 sea bream fillets
- 2 salmon fillets
- 70 g of shrimp
- 350 g of mussels
- 4 eggs
- 30 cl of fresh cream
- 20 g of fresh tarragon
- 2 pinches of salt
- 2 pinches of pepper

Separately, cook the sea bream fillets, salmon, shrimp, and mussels. Set them aside.

Preheat your oven to 120°C.

Coarsely blend the sea bream fillets with half of the eggs and fresh cream. Add half of the tarragon, salt, and pepper.

Do the same with the salmon and the remaining half of the eggs, cream, tarragon, salt, and pepper.

Line your cake mold with cling film and layer the salmon mixture, then the shrimp, then the mussels, and finally the sea bream mixture.

Press lightly to compact the preparation.

Place the mold in a stainless steel tray and add 1 cm of water to the bottom to create a bain-marie.

Place everything in your oven for 20 minutes.

Let it cool and refrigerate for 4 hours.

Carefully unmold onto a serving dish, and optionally decorate the top with thin slices of lemon cut in half before serving.

You can accompany this terrine with cocktail sauce, aioli, or lemon mayonnaise.

Consider adding a nice leaf of lettuce or lamb's lettuce.

Seafood Velouté with Pastis

For 4 people:

Clean 1 kg of mussels thoroughly.

Slice 100 g of squid.

Chop 1 onion and brown it in a pot with 1 tablespoon of olive oil.

Add the mussels and 10 cl of Pastis.

Cook over medium heat, covered, until the mussels open.

Remove from heat and wait a few minutes before discarding the shells.

Strain the cooking juice through a sieve.

To prepare the velouté:

In a saucepan, pour 1 liter of fish stock.

Add 200 g of sweet potato and 1 tablespoon of Herbes de Provence.

Bring to a boil and cook for 20 minutes.

Add the strained mussel cooking juice.

Blend everything and season to taste with salt, pepper, and 7 g of saffron.

Now add 100 g of peeled shrimp and 100 g of squid. Bring to a simmer.

Add the mussels and 10 cl of crème fraîche.

Cook for a few minutes, stirring with a wooden spoon to achieve a perfect, creamy mixture.

 Serve the velouté in deep plates.

Feel free to accompany it with garlic croutons.

Perfect Pairing Ideas:
  ☆ *Fresh chopped coriander.*
  ☆ *A few drops of Tabasco®.*
  ☆ *Grilled lemon zest.*

Frog Legs with Maître d'Hôtel Butter

You might say, nothing exceptional. Except that I have deboned them all to keep only the flesh. Placed in a mold and accompanied by Maître d'Hôtel butter, <u>BUT</u> in a pomade form.

Ingredients:

- 500 g of frog legs
- 100 g of butter
- 2 cloves of garlic
- 1 bunch of parsley
- 1 lemon
- Salt and pepper

Prepare the Maître d'Hôtel butter in a mixing bowl by adding half of the butter, chopped garlic, salt, pepper, and chopped parsley.

Work the butter with a fork, mixing all the ingredients until it reaches a pomade consistency.

Place the pomade on parchment paper and shape it into a log about 5 to 6 cm in diameter.

Refrigerate the log.

Rinse the frog legs in cold water and dry them with paper towels.

Melt the remaining butter in a large pan over medium heat.

When the butter turns nut-brown, add the frog legs and cook them for about 3-4 minutes on each side until they are golden. Season with salt and pepper. Remove them from the pan, drain, and set aside.

The longest part is now! Debone each leg to keep only the flesh. Be careful with the tiny bones. This preparation requires attention and patience.

For serving, place the frog leg flesh in the oven to reheat. Then place the preparation in a mold in the center of a plate.

On top, place a slice of Maître d'Hôtel butter about 1 cm thick.

Add a drizzle of lemon juice and serve with lemon wedges and fresh parsley.

Feel free to let your imagination run wild. For example, add to your preparation: bread croutons, bacon bits, Espelette pepper, Pastis, and why not hazelnuts, tomato confit, or apple pieces.

Basil Shrimp Skewers

Start by preparing a Basil Sauce.

Ingredients:

- 1 bunch of fresh basil
- 2 cloves of garlic
- 1 teaspoon of ground cumin
- 1 teaspoon of salt
- 2 tablespoons of white wine vinegar
- 100 ml of olive oil

Wash and dry the basil. Peel the garlic cloves. Put everything in a blender and add the cumin, salt, and vinegar.

Blend until you get a smooth paste.

Slowly add the olive oil while continuing to blend until the sauce is well emulsified and smooth.

Taste and adjust the salt or vinegar according to your preferences.

Set aside.

Prepare your skewers.

On a wooden skewer, alternate a shrimp, a cherry tomato, a slice of chorizo, a piece of onion, a piece of red bell pepper, and finish with a shrimp.

Season with salt and pepper.

Generally, for an appetizer, 2 skewers like this per person will suffice. Adjust the quantity according to your guests.

Cook your skewers in a pan or on a griddle for 2 minutes on each side.

Place them on a dish and brush them with your warm basil sauce.

Garnish with a few fresh basil leaves and serve.

Be careful not to overheat the basil sauce; it should be warm so that it does not break down.

If you choose to enjoy this excellent recipe as a main dish, you can accompany it with baked potatoes topped with basil sauce.

For those who love a bit of heat, add a few drops of chili to your sauce.

Scallop Carpaccio with Smoked Salmon Ice Cream

Prepare your smoked salmon ice cream.

Blend 200 g of smoked salmon with 20 cl of thick crème fraîche, 10 cl of milk, and 1 tablespoon of lemon juice until smooth. Season with salt and pepper.

Pour the mixture into an ice cream maker and churn for 20-25 minutes until the ice cream is creamy.

Transfer to the freezer.

For the carpaccio:

Rinse the scallops under cold water and pat them dry with paper towels. Slice them thinly with a sharp knife.

Arrange the scallop slices on a plate. Drizzle with lemon juice and olive oil. Season with salt and pepper.

Let marinate in the refrigerator for about 15 minutes.

For serving, arrange the marinated scallop slices on plates. Add a scoop of smoked salmon ice cream in the center of each plate and sprinkle with chopped chives and a few lamb's lettuce leaves.

My Meats

Slow-Cooked Pork Shank with Caramelized Onions and Whole-Grain Mustard

For 4 people, choose 4 beautiful pork shanks.

In a pressure cooker, pour about 10 cl of olive oil and heat over medium heat.

Place your shanks in the cooker and brown them on all sides.

Deglaze with 20 cl of fruity white wine. Let simmer for 5 minutes, then add 30 cl of meat broth.

Bring to a boil, then cover the cooker and let it steam for 25 minutes over low heat.

Turn off the heat and let the steam escape.

Preheat your oven to 150°C (fan-assisted).

In a clay dish, place and align your shanks.

In the broth, add 2 tablespoons of sweet Spanish paprika, salt, and pepper. Pour this broth into your dish to halfway up the shanks.

Put in the oven. It's time for 3 hours of cooking.

Turn your shanks every 30 minutes so they soak well in the broth. If necessary, add more broth that you have previously simmered.

The cooking is finished when your shanks have a tender consistency.

For serving:

Place the equivalent of 2 tablespoons of caramelized onions on the shank, then a layer of whole-grain mustard.

Put in the oven just long enough to warm up and serve immediately.

Some potatoes cooked in pork fat will enhance your shanks. Think about it!

Free-Range Chicken Fillet Ballotine with Fresh Mushrooms and Serrano Ham

Ingredients:

- 4 free-range chicken fillets
- 200g of fresh mushrooms, sliced
- 4 slices of Serrano ham
- Olive oil
- Salt and pepper

Open your chicken fillets and flatten them using a rolling pin.

Sear them in a hot pan with olive oil for 4 to 5 seconds on each side.

Lay them flat on your work surface. Season with crushed five-pepper blend.

Place the chicken fillets on a piece of plastic wrap. Along the length of each fillet, line up the sliced mushrooms.

Finally, cover with a slice of Serrano ham.

Roll the chicken fillets using the plastic wrap, tightening well to form ballotines. Tie them with kitchen string.

Start cooking in cold water in a large saucepan. Bring to a boil and cook for about 10 minutes.

For serving:

Cut the ballotines into slices about 4 to 5 cm thick.

Place them on a baking sheet and bake until they are well heated.

Plate and sprinkle with chopped parsley before serving.

Be careful with the salt. The Serrano ham will add its own saltiness.

Serve with a good mushroom sauce.

Accompany your chicken ballotines with steamed vegetables, potatoes, or rice.

Chicken Blanquette with Black Truffle

Ingredients:

- 600 g of chicken breasts
- 200 g of sliced button mushrooms
- 100 g of bacon bits
- 200 g of onions
- 1 carrot
- 1 chicken bouillon cube
- 30 g of flour
- 50 g of butter
- 2 tablespoons of thick cream
- 1 egg yolk
- 1 lemon (for the juice)
- Salt and pepper
- 40 g of fresh truffle

Preparation:

In a large pot, bring 1.5 liters of salted water to a boil with the chicken bouillon cube.

Add the chicken pieces and the carrot cut into slices, and cook for 15 minutes. Drain and reserve the broth.

In a Dutch oven, melt 20 g of butter. Add the sliced onions and bacon bits, and sauté until golden.

Add the sliced mushrooms and cook until tender.

In another saucepan, melt the remaining butter.

Add the flour and stir for 2 minutes to make a white roux.

Gradually add half of the chicken cooking broth, stirring constantly to obtain a smooth sauce.

Pour this sauce into the Dutch oven with the vegetables and bacon bits. Add the chicken pieces.

Season with salt and pepper.

Simmer over low heat for about 30 minutes, until the chicken is well cooked and tender.

In a bowl, mix the thick cream, egg yolk, lemon juice, and chopped truffle.

Add this mixture to the Dutch oven off the heat and mix well to bind the sauce.

Plate and top with 3 or 4 slices of fresh truffle and sprinkle with chopped parsley.

Serve hot.

Beef Tartare on Toasted Garlic Brioche

Start by making the tartar sauce (see recipe below) to which you will add 2 tablespoons of ketchup and a few drops of Tabasco®.

In a bowl, place 500 g of finely chopped beef fillet.

Mix thoroughly with the tartar sauce.

Place the mixture in a ring mold on a beautiful slice of brioche that you have previously toasted by rubbing it with garlic and drizzling with olive oil.

Press lightly and top with finely chopped red onions, a pinch of lemon zest, and half a sun-dried tomato. Drizzle with a little olive oil.

Serve this dish with potatoes sautéed in beef fat. Delicious!

Quail Fillets with Cognac-Soaked Raisins

This recipe is very simple but requires a bit of preparation before serving your quail fillets.

Three or four days before your meal, place your quail fillets in olive oil to marinate. Add salt, pepper, and an aromatic herb of your choice.

In another container, cover 50 g of raisins with good quality cognac.

Prepare a rich meat jus by adding the cognac-soaked raisins and 3 tablespoons of the cognac marinade. Heat over low heat until it begins to simmer.

Sear your fillets in a pan or on a griddle. Arrange them on your plate and drizzle with the meat jus and raisins.

Quail fillets are best enjoyed seared. Do not overcook them.

An excellent potato flan will accompany your quail fillets perfectly.

Confit Duck Leg

Rub the duck legs with coarse salt.

Place them in a dish, add 4 crushed garlic cloves, thyme, and bay leaves.

Cover and let rest in the refrigerator for 24 hours.

The next day, rinse the duck legs to remove the excess salt. Dry them thoroughly with a clean cloth.

Melt the duck fat in a large pot over low heat.

Add the duck legs, ensuring they are completely submerged in the fat.

Cook over very low heat for about 3 hours. The meat should be tender and easily come off the bone.

Once cooked, you can store the duck legs in the cooking fat. Place them in an airtight jar, cover with fat, and keep in the refrigerator. They will keep for several weeks.

To serve, heat the duck legs in a pan over medium heat until they are golden and crispy.

Thinly Sliced Raw Rump Steak Marinated in Pedro Ximénez and Espelette Pepper

For 4 servings, choose a piece of rump steak about 18 cm long and 6 to 7 cm in diameter.

Sear it in hot olive oil for about 2 minutes on all sides. The surface should be slightly crusted.

Let it cool.

Then, cut into thin slices barely 2 millimeters thick and arrange them on a plate, slices side by side.

Sprinkle with finely sliced red onion. Add cherry tomatoes and sliced button mushrooms.

Season with quality coarse salt and crushed pepper.

Drizzle sparingly with Pedro Ximénez sauce and finish by sprinkling with Espelette pepper.

Serve at room temperature.

My Fish

Mussels with Seafood Cream, Bacon, and Roquefort

Ingredients:

- 2 kg of mussels
- 200 g of bacon bits
- 1 onion
- 50 cl of thick fresh cream
- 100 g of Roquefort cheese
- A pinch of Espelette pepper
- Fresh chopped parsley

Clean the mussels.

Rinse them thoroughly under cold water.

In a large pot, sauté the bacon bits and onion until golden.

Add the mussels to the pot and cook over high heat until they open.

Remove them with a slotted spoon and set aside.
Preparation of the sauce:

Reduce the heat and add the fresh cream to the pot.

Add the crumbled Roquefort and let it melt while stirring. Season with a pinch of Espelette pepper.

Return the mussels to the pot and mix well to coat them with the sauce.

Let simmer over low heat for a few minutes.

Sprinkle with fresh chopped parsley before serving.

Fisherman's Platter

Ingredients:

- Fish of the day (about 200g per person)
- Mussels (500g)
- Squid (200g)
- Cockles (300g)
- Shrimp (200g)
- Chorizo (100g, sliced)
- Garlic (2 cloves, chopped)
- Onion (1, finely chopped)
- Tomatoes (2, peeled and chopped)
- White wine (200ml)
- Fish stock (200ml)
- Fresh cream (100ml)
- Parsley (a few sprigs, chopped)
- Olive oil

Preparation:

Clean the mussels and cockles. Cook them over high heat in a large pot with a bit of white wine until they open. Set aside.

Peel the shrimp and clean the squid, then cut the squid into rings.

Cooking the Fish:

In a pan, heat some olive oil and cook the fish of the day until golden and cooked through. Set aside.

Preparing the Sauce:

In a large pan, sauté the garlic and onion in olive oil until translucent.

Add the chorizo slices and cook for a few minutes.

Stir in the chopped tomatoes and let simmer for 5 minutes.

Pour in the white wine and fish stock, then reduce by half.

Add the fresh cream and mix well. Season with salt and pepper.

Assembly:

Add the squid, shrimp, mussels, and cockles to the sauce.

Let simmer for 5 to 7 minutes until the seafood is well cooked.

Gently incorporate the fish of the day to avoid breaking it.

Sprinkle with chopped parsley before serving.
Serve this Fisherman's Platter hot, accompanied by rice.

 You can spice up your dish with some chili.

Sole and Scallop Paupiettes

Ingredients:

- 4 sole fillets
- 4 scallops without roe
- 100 ml of fresh cream
- 100 ml of dry white wine
- 2 shallots, finely chopped
- 50 g of butter
- A few sprigs of chopped parsley
- Salt and pepper

Preparation of the Paupiettes:

Lay the sole fillets flat on a board. Place a scallop in the center of each fillet.

Roll the sole fillets around the scallops to form paupiettes and tie them with kitchen string.

Melt the butter in a pan over medium heat. Add the shallots and sauté until translucent.

Add the sole paupiettes and lightly brown them on each side.

Pour the white wine into the pan and reduce by half.

Add the fresh cream, salt, and pepper. Simmer over low heat for about 10 minutes, until the paupiettes are well cooked.

Remove the paupiettes from the pan and place them on a dish.

Reduce the sauce if necessary, then pour it over the paupiettes. Sprinkle with chopped parsley before serving.

Serve these sole paupiettes stuffed with scallops with a side of steamed vegetables or rice.

Langoustines with Shrimp Cream

Ingredients:

- 1 kg of langoustines
- 500 g of shrimp
- 1 onion
- 2 cloves of garlic
- 25 cl of fresh cream
- 20 cl of dry white wine
- 50 g of butter
- 1 bouquet garni (thyme, bay leaf, parsley)
- Salt and pepper

Preparation of the Langoustines and Shrimp:

Shell the langoustines and shrimp, keeping the heads and shells.

Finely blend the shrimp in a food processor.

In a saucepan, brown the butter, chopped onion, and minced garlic.

Add the shells and cook for 6 to 7 minutes.

Deglaze with the white wine and reduce by half.

Add the bouquet garni and 1 liter of water. Simmer over low heat for 30 minutes.

Strain the broth through a fine sieve to remove the heads and shells.

Return the filtered broth to the saucepan and add the blended shrimp.

Add the fresh cream to the broth and reduce over low heat until creamy.

Season with salt and pepper.

Cook the langoustines in the sauce and simmer over low heat for 5 minutes.

Serve hot, accompanied by fragrant basmati rice.

Mussels Vol-au-Vent with Seafood Sauce

Ingredients:

- 2 kg of mussels
- 250 g of peeled shrimp
- 200 g of scallops
- 1 onion
- 2 shallots
- 2 cloves of garlic
- 30 cl of fresh cream
- 20 cl of dry white wine
- 50 g of butter
- 1 bouquet garni (thyme, bay leaf, parsley)
- 4 vol-au-vent pastry shells
- Salt and pepper

Clean the mussels and cook them over high heat with the white wine until they open. Drain them, reserving the cooking juice.

Shell the mussels.

In a large pan, melt the butter and sauté the chopped onion, shallots, and garlic until translucent.

Add the seafood: shrimp and scallops, and cook for a few minutes.

Then add the shelled mussels.

Preparing the Sauce:

Add the filtered mussel cooking juice and reduce.

Stir in the fresh cream and simmer over low heat until the sauce thickens.

Season with salt and pepper.

Warm the vol-au-vent pastry shells in the oven.

Fill them with the seafood mixture and sauce.

Serve hot, garnished with fresh chopped parsley.

My Homemade Sauces

Mayonnaise

Ingredients for 4 servings:

- 1 egg yolk
- 1 tablespoon of Dijon mustard
- 25 cl of sunflower oil
- 1 teaspoon of wine vinegar
- Salt

In a mixing bowl, combine the egg yolk, mustard, and salt.

Gradually pour in the oil while whisking vigorously until you achieve a thick emulsion.

Add the vinegar and whisk again. It's ready!

 All ingredients should be at room temperature.

You can replace sunflower oil with corn oil.

Traditionally, mayonnaise is not peppered to avoid black specks.

Lemon Mayonnaise

For the mayonnaise recipe, use only 20 cl of sunflower oil, omit the vinegar, and add 5 cl of lemon juice at the end of the emulsion.

Aïoli

Being committed to preserving gastronomy, I present to you the traditional recipe for aïoli. This article was written by Gwennaëlle Vidal, published on June 10, 2024, and featured on the «cuisineAZ» website.

Aïoli is a specialty originating from the Mediterranean basin, deeply rooted in Provençal and Spanish culinary heritage.

Originally, it was an emulsion of garlic and olive oil, resulting from grinding in a mortar and pestle, used to season seafood, snails, or potatoes. Nowadays, it is often enriched with egg yolk, lemon juice, or even milk or bread crumbs, making it more like garlic mayonnaise.

Aïoli is typically served with a variety of steamed vegetables, poached fish, and seafood.

Traditional Aïoli Recipe

Ingredients (for 1 bowl):

- 1 egg yolk
- 4 cloves of garlic
- 20 cl of olive oil
- 1 teaspoon of lemon juice
- A pinch of salt

Preparation

Place the egg yolk, crushed garlic cloves, and salt in a bowl. Add a few drops of olive oil and start whisking the mixture gently.

Continue to incorporate the olive oil drop by drop for the first 10 minutes to thicken the sauce (otherwise, it will remain liquid and difficult to fix), whisking after each addition.

Once half of the oil is added, the base should have thickened. You can then increase the pace by adding the oil in 2 cl doses.

Add the lemon juice at the very end of the preparation to smooth and refresh the sauce.

TIP: Aïoli is always more flavorful when consumed the same day. For bacteriological reasons, it is recommended to finish it within 24 hours of preparation, at most within 48 hours (the lemon juice slightly prolongs its preservation). Be sure to cover it well and store it in the coldest part of the fridge, keeping it at a temperature of 4°C or lower.

Cocktail Sauce

Ingredients for 4 servings:

- 1 egg yolk
- 1 tablespoon of Dijon mustard
- 25 cl of sunflower oil
- 1 teaspoon of wine vinegar
- 4 drops of piri-piri
- 30 g of ketchup
- 1.5 cl of pastis
- Salt

In a mixing bowl, combine the egg yolk, mustard, and salt.

Gradually pour in the oil while whisking vigorously until you achieve a thick emulsion. Add the ketchup, piri-piri, vinegar, and pastis. Whisk again. It's ready!

 All ingredients should be at room temperature.

You can replace sunflower oil with corn oil.

You can replace pastis with whisky or cognac.

Sauce for My Tuna Tartare

Peel, blend, and place 160 g of onion in a mixing bowl.

Add 40 g of finely chopped pickles and 40 g of finely chopped capers.

Then, mix everything with 2 tablespoons of mayonnaise, 1 tablespoon of powdered sugar, salt, pepper, a few drops of chili, and 1 teaspoon of Dijon mustard.

Taste and adjust the seasoning.

Cola Sauce

Always in search of innovation, I once decided to make a cola sauce. To my surprise, it turned out perfectly and was excellent.

Here is my (super easy) recipe:

In a saucepan, make a blond roux with 20 g of butter and 20 g of flour.

Keep on low heat and gradually pour in your cola drink until it reaches the consistency of a sauce. Whisk vigorously.

Add 1 tablespoon of fresh cream.

To give it a kick, I added a pinch of five-peppercorn blend.

Carefully control your heat and cooking to prevent your sauce from turning into caramel.

This sauce pairs wonderfully with white meat.

Port and Honey Sauce

Ingredients:

- 1 onion, finely chopped
- 2 tablespoons of butter
- 200 ml of red port
- 3 tablespoons of honey
- 200 ml of veal stock
- 100 ml of fresh cream
- 1 tablespoon of cornstarch (optional, for thickening)
- Salt and pepper

In a saucepan, melt the butter over medium heat.

Add the chopped onion and sauté until translucent.

Pour the port into the saucepan and add the honey.

Let simmer for about 5 minutes to evaporate the alcohol and blend the flavors.

Add the veal stock and simmer for another 10 minutes.

Stir in the fresh cream and mix well.

Season with salt and pepper to taste.

Let simmer for a few more minutes until the sauce reaches the desired consistency.

If you want a thicker sauce, dissolve the cornstarch in a bit of cold water and add it to the sauce.

This sauce is perfect for accompanying red meats, such as beef fillet or duck breast.

Green Peppercorn Sauce

For 2 people:

In a saucepan, make a blond roux with 20 g of butter and 20 g of flour.

Pour in ¼ liter of cold water in which you have dissolved ½ bouillon cube, all at once.

Bring to a simmer while whisking and add ½ teaspoon of ground green peppercorns.

Control the thickness and, if needed, thin with more bouillon.

At the end, add a tablespoon of fresh cream and a few fresh green peppercorns.

Adapt your bouillon cube according to your dish. Chicken, vegetable, beef bouillon, etc.

Be careful with the salt, as bouillon cubes usually contain enough.

Instead of a blond roux, you can opt for a brown roux.

Mushroom Sauce

For 2 people:

Thinly slice 100 g of Paris mushrooms and sweat them in a pan until they start to dry. Set aside.

In a saucepan, make a blond roux with 20 g of butter and 20 g of flour.

Moisten with 2 dl of vegetable broth and add the mushrooms you just cooked at the same time.

Whisk vigorously and when your sauce is thickened, add 1 tablespoon of fresh cream. Check the consistency and, if necessary, thin the sauce with more broth.

Finally, add 50 g of mushrooms cut into small cubes. Season with salt and pepper to taste.

Orange Sauce

For 2 people:

Zest one orange.

Squeeze ¼ liter of orange juice.

In a saucepan, make a blond roux with 20 g of butter and 20 g of flour.

Add the orange juice and bring to a simmer while whisking.

Control the smoothness and, if necessary, thin with more orange juice.

At the end, add one tablespoon of fresh cream and the orange zest.

Pepper to taste.

Mango Velouté

This velouté is very easy to make as it simply requires blending the pulp of a mango and thinning it with a bit of water, fresh cream, and a few centiliters of lemon juice.

I use it to accompany a lightly cooked salmon and flavor it with a hint of Espelette pepper and chopped fresh parsley.

Asturian Cider Sauce

Prepare ½ finely chopped shallot, 420 g of butter, 35 cl of Asturian cider, 10 cl of fresh cream, 25 g of bacon bits, salt, and pepper.

In your saucepan, melt the butter and add the finely chopped shallot and bacon bits.

Once everything is well browned, pour the cider into the saucepan and let it reduce for 15 minutes over medium heat.

Add the fresh cream and let it simmer over low heat for about 10 minutes, stirring and monitoring your sauce.

Season with salt and pepper.

This sauce is ideal for accompanying white meats. I serve it with pork tenderloin.

Meat Jus with Mushrooms and Port

Ingredients:

- 500 ml of chicken broth
- 200 ml of port
- 200 g of sliced button mushrooms
- 2 finely chopped shallots
- 2 minced garlic cloves
- 2 tablespoons of butter
- 1 tablespoon of flour
- 1 tablespoon of tomato paste
- Salt and pepper
- A pinch of Herbes de Provence

Preparation:

Heat one tablespoon of butter in a pan.

Add the shallots and garlic, and sauté over low heat until translucent.

Add the sliced mushrooms and cook until tender. Set aside.

In a saucepan, melt the remaining butter. Add the flour and mix well to make a roux. Cook for a few minutes without browning.

Deglaze with the port by pouring it into the saucepan and reduce by half, stirring constantly.

Add the chicken broth, tomato paste, and a pinch of Herbes de Provence.

Bring to a boil, then reduce the heat and simmer for about 15 minutes.

Add the cooked mushrooms to the sauce and simmer for another 5 minutes.

Season with salt and pepper to taste.

Serve hot with your favorite meat.

Lemon and Tarragon Sauce

In a saucepan, melt 20 g of butter over low heat. Sweat 1 finely chopped shallot in the butter.

Deglaze with 15 cl of white wine and let reduce for 4 minutes.

Add 20 g of sifted flour and stir vigorously to avoid lumps.

Add 25 cl of fish stock, 25 g of chopped fresh tarragon, and 5 cl of lemon juice.

Whisk and add 10 cl of fresh cream at the last moment.

Season with salt and pepper to taste.

To soften the acidic taste of the lemon, which can be aggressive on the palate, feel free to add 1 teaspoon of powdered sugar to your sauce. Be careful not to caramelize it during cooking.

Horchata de Chuffa Sauce

Horchata de chufa (Spanish spelling of the Valencian expression orxata de xufa), sometimes translated into French as "orgeat de souchet," is an opaque, whitish drink reminiscent of milk (and thus often considered a form of plant milk) in appearance and color. It is made from water, tiger nut tubers (chufa in Spanish), and most often, sugar. This drink is typical of the Valencian community in Spain, where it is very popular. It is sometimes served with crushed ice (granizado). Traditionally, it is enjoyed with sweet buns called fartons.

(Wikipédia)

Make a white roux with one tablespoon of flour and one tablespoon of butter. As soon as it is ready, pour in 20 cl of horchata.

Control the thickness of your sauce and, if necessary, add a little more horchata to thin it out.

✋ *It pairs ideally with grilled white meats, rice, pasta, and grilled vegetables. In this case, add a pinch of crushed pepper to your sauce.*

Use it sweet to accompany crepes, waffles, pastries like cake or pound cake.

Potato Side Dishes

Homemade Mashed Potatoes

Wash 250 kg of potatoes and place them in a pot. Cover them with cold water.

Add 5 g of salt and bring to a boil for about 25 minutes. When the blade of your knife easily pierces the potatoes, they are ready.

Drain them and, while they are still warm, peel them.

You can now mash them very finely.

Put your mashed potatoes back in the pot and, over low heat, stir to dry them slightly.

Boil 10 cl of milk and pour it over the mashed potatoes, adding 65 g of butter cut into small cubes. Whisk vigorously. Adjust the seasoning and serve immediately.

✋ *The potato varieties Artemis, Bintje, Marabel, Manon, and Caesar are ideal for making mashed potatoes as they are easy to mash. Conversely, Joël Robuchon used BF15.*

Traditionally, mashed potatoes are not peppered to avoid black specks. It's a visual preference!

Gratin Dauphinois

Thinly slice your potatoes.

Place them in a mixing bowl, add salt, ground pepper, grated nutmeg, a beaten egg, boiled milk, and grated Gruyère cheese. Mix everything thoroughly.

Pour this mixture into a garlic-rubbed and well-buttered dish.

Generously cover the surface with grated Gruyère cheese and add a few pieces of butter.

Bake for 40 minutes.

Creamy Potato Flan

Preheat your oven to 180°C (350°F).

Peel 1 kg of potatoes and cut them into thin slices.

Cook them in a large pot of boiling salted water for about 10 minutes, until they are tender but still firm.

Drain and set aside.

In a skillet, melt 50 g of butter and sauté 2 finely chopped shallots and 2 minced garlic cloves until they are translucent.

In a large bowl, beat 3 eggs, 200 ml of milk, and 200 ml of heavy cream.

Season with salt, pepper, and a pinch of Espelette pepper if you want a bit of a kick.

Butter a gratin dish and place a layer of potatoes at the bottom.

Add some of the shallots and garlic, then sprinkle with grated cheese.

Repeat the layers until all ingredients are used, finishing with a layer of grated cheese.

Pour the egg-cream-milk mixture over the potatoes.

Bake the gratin dish for about 30 to 40 minutes, until the flan is golden and set.

Let it rest for a few minutes before serving.

This creamy potato flan is perfect as a side dish for meat or poultry.

Lyonnaise Potatoes

Boil your potatoes in water. Drain and peel them.

Now, cut them into slices and sauté them in butter in a skillet.

Also, sauté a finely chopped onion in butter until it turns golden brown.

Add the onions to the sautéed potatoes and season with salt and pepper.

Sauté the mixture for 2 to 3 minutes to blend the flavors. Voilà, it's done!

✋ *For 1 kg of potatoes, you will need ¼ of that weight in onions (1 kg of potatoes = 250 g of onions).*

Potato Churros

In a large mixing bowl, combine 45 cl of milk with 200 g of flour and 200 g of previously cooked mashed potatoes. Salt the mixture and let it rest for 10 minutes.

Meanwhile, heat 2 liters of sunflower oil in a large saucepan.

Pour your batter into a piping bag and when the oil reaches 180°C, pipe churros about 10 cm long into the oil. Let them brown for about 3 minutes before removing them from the saucepan and draining them.

Serve them immediately while hot.

Homestyle Potatoes

Peel your potatoes and cook them in salted water.

When they are perfectly cooked, drain and mash them with a fork.

Season with salt and pepper, then add chopped chives and a bit of boiling milk. Mix thoroughly.

With this "potato dough," form balls the size of an egg, then flatten them with the palm of your hand to give them the shape of small patties.

Coat them in flour and brown them on both sides in butter or olive oil.

 You can add a beaten egg to this mixture.

Parisian Potatoes

Scoop out small, round potatoes using a melon baller, about the size of a small hazelnut.

Lightly salt them and cook slowly in butter. Keep them tender and golden.

At the end of cooking, roll them in melted and buttered meat glaze.

My Desserts

Red Fruit Sangria Cup

Place 300 ml of your sangria in a mixing bowl. After softening, add 1 and a half sheets of gelatin. Make sure it is well dissolved and divide it evenly into 6 cups.

Chill overnight to allow the sangria to set properly.

Prepare your desserts by adding:

- 1 generous tablespoon of fruits (red fruits, strawberries, raspberries, etc.)
- Then, a scoop of vanilla ice cream
- A red fruit coulis
- Whipped cream

Coconut Rice Pudding

End your meal on a sweet and exotic note.

Ingredients:

- 200 g round rice
- 1 can of coconut milk (400 ml)
- 50 cl milk
- 100 g grated coconut
- 3 tablespoons sugar
- 1 vanilla pod
- 2 cl water

Boil a pot of water and immerse the rice for 2 minutes. Drain and rinse it.

Split the vanilla pod in half and place it in a saucepan with the milk, coconut milk, 70 g of grated coconut, and water. Bring to a boil.

Add the rice to the saucepan and cook over low heat for about 20 minutes, stirring occasionally.

Incorporate the sugar and let simmer for another ten minutes or until the milk is almost completely absorbed.

Remove from heat and pour the rice pudding into ramekins.

Let cool, then sprinkle with the remaining grated coconut before placing in the refrigerator.

Thank you Mémé

Barraquito

Well!!! Obviously, I didn't invent this. But I find this coffee so amazing and delicious that I also offer it in my restaurant. And very often, my customers take it as a dessert.

Some explanations about this special coffee:

The Barraquito or Zaperoco is a sweet coffee drink very popular in the Canary Islands, Spain. It is often served in layers, thanks to the different densities of its ingredients, which are, from bottom to top, condensed milk, liqueur, espresso, and frothy milk. It is served in a medium or large glass and garnished with cinnamon powder and lemon or lime zest. The liqueur is usually Licor 43, a sweet liqueur flavored with forty-three spices, or Tía María, a Jamaican coffee liqueur with a slight touch of vanilla. There is also a non-alcoholic version.

In the northern part of the island, the area between Buenavista in the west and Puerto de la Cruz in the east, it is also known as "Zaperoco." In the region of Santa Cruz and La Laguna, Barraquito refers to a coffee with condensed milk and whole milk, which in other places is called Leche-leche, similar to a café bombón.

Origin

There are several theories, although the most accepted one dates back to the middle of the last century in Santa Cruz. According to the Diccionario histórico-etimológico del habla canaria by Marcial Morera, the name comes from a regular customer of the Bar Imperial, Don Sebastián Rubio, nicknamed "Barraquito" or "Barraco", who always ordered a cortado with condensed milk in a long glass, a glass of Licor 43, a lemon zest, and cinnamon. This bar is still active and is located near Plaza de la Paz. According to other sources, this happened at Bar Paragüitas, also in Santa Cruz.

It is also said that it was invented by the bartender Don Manolo Grijalbo (kioskero according to others), from an establishment near the Marquesina del Puerto, a place that served as a meeting point for artists, businessmen, students, etc.

Whatever its origin, the Barraquito quickly spread throughout the islands, but it is unknown on the mainland.

Wikipédia

Barragusto

And from there, the idea came to me to make it a dessert. My famous Barragusto, named in reference to my restaurant.

Here is my recipe, strictly following the ingredients of the Barraquito Canario.

For 6 servings:

Dissolve 1 and a half sheets of gelatin in 180 ml of Licor 43. Divide the alcohol evenly among your 6 servings.

Let set overnight.

Prepare your coffee mousse:

Heat ½ liter of heavy cream, mixing in 5 tablespoons of instant coffee.

Separate the whites and yolks of 3 eggs.

Whisk the yolks with 100 g of sugar until pale, then incorporate the coffee cream.

Thicken over low heat, stirring constantly. The cream should coat your spoon. Let cool.

Beat the egg whites with a pinch of salt until stiff peaks form.

Gently fold them into the cold coffee cream using a spatula.

Take your chilled servings out of the refrigerator and pour in the equivalent of 1 tablespoon of condensed milk.

Top with the coffee mousse.

Refrigerate and let set for at least 8 hours.

When ready to serve, pipe whipped cream on top in a rosette shape.

Finally, garnish with a lemon zest and a pinch of ground cinnamon.

Tarte Tatin

Ingredients for 6 to 8 people:

- 8 to 10 apples
- 150 g butter
- 150 g de granulated sugar
- 200 g de shortcrust pastry

Peel the apples, remove the cores, and cut the apples into eighths.

In a Tatin tart pan, melt the butter and sprinkle with granulated sugar. Stir with a wooden spoon until you get a brown caramel. Remove from heat and set aside.

In a skillet, add part of the butter, sugar, and half of the apples. Let them brown without burning for about ten minutes over low heat, stirring gently to avoid breaking the fruit. When they have lost their hardness and crunch, they are ready!

Arrange this first batch of apples, well packed and tight, in the pan in a rosette shape. Pour the equivalent of 2 to 3 tablespoons of caramel over the apples.

Repeat the same operation with the rest of the apples, butter, and sugar, and form the second layer of your tart.

Bake your tart in the oven preheated to 150°C for 20 minutes. Remove and let cool.

Then, on the apples, gently place your 4 mm thick pastry, slightly larger in diameter than the pan. Using your fingers, tuck the edges of the pastry into the inner side of the pan.

With the tip of a paring knife, make a small chimney to allow steam to escape during baking.

Return to the oven and bake for 20 to 25 minutes until the pastry is perfectly cooked.

Remove the pan from the oven and let cool for about 30 minutes. You can now cover it with a plate and turn it over.

Admire this masterpiece of French pastry!

Make sure to pack the apples tightly together as they will shrink during cooking.

Depending on your taste, you can sprinkle your Tarte Tatin with cinnamon. It pairs perfectly with fresh cream or a scoop of vanilla ice cream.

Try it also with puff pastry.

Legends around Tarte Tatin
Source: Wikipedia

The upside-down pie is mentioned in 1790. La Tradition: revue générale des contes, légendes in 1906 cites the expression "When it happens that, of two sisters, the younger marries before the elder, the latter is made to eat an upside-down pie, hence the following expression: "*A' li ont fait manger de le tarte àrtournée*"".

At the end of the 19th century, the tart of the sisters Stéphanie (1838-1917) and Caroline Tatin (1847-1911), hoteliers in Lamotte-Beuvron in Sologne, was famous throughout the region. A manuscript by the teacher Marie Souchon indicates that they got the recipe from the anonymous cook of Count Alfred Leblanc de Chatauvillard.

On December 18, 1899, the Parisian daily "Le Journal" recounted on the front page the arrival of the famous tart at the end of the meal:

> «*The pitch rises, bursts, fills the bright room, until the moment when, in the midst of general joy and the excitement of satisfied but not satiated stomachs, appears, at the fingertips of the servant, Mlle Tatin's tart. The Burgundy has circulated; the brains are light and the souls communicative. A cry of satisfaction comes from all chests, a joy of the eyes goes ahead of the triumphant tart. It is cut, served, swallowed.* »

The Hôtel Tatin, opposite the station, was frequented by many hunters. A legend has it that one Sunday at the opening of the hunting season, while preparing an apple tart for a hunters' meal, Stéphanie, in the heat of the moment, forgot to put a pastry in the pan and simply baked it with apples. Realizing her mistake, she decided to simply add the pastry on top of the apples and bake the tart that way.

Marie Souchon's recipe was published, apparently for the first time, in 1921 by the Solognot poet Paul Besnard in a local magazine Blois et le Loir-et-Cher with the requirement to use a copper dish.

The recipe appears in Le Livret d'or de la section gastronomique régionaliste du Salon d'automne de 1923 under the direction of Austin de Croze with the title Recette solognote: Tarte des Demoiselles Tatin, de Lamotte-Beuvron. It was reprinted with the same title in December of the same year in Comœdia, without a signature but with the same insistence on the obligation to use a copper mold.

The recipe appears in La France gastronomique - L'Orléanais (1926) by Curnonsky and Marcel Rouff.

The recipe was published in Paris-soir on August 25, 1929.

In 1931, Hubert Fillay transcribed the recipe that Paul Besnard got from the Tatin sisters in La Dépêche du Berry (the only original readable online) and specified that the best apple for this tart is the yellow reinette with red veins.

A second legend has it that Curnonsky launched the trend in 1926 and invented the legend of one of the sisters' clumsiness. No text by Curnonsky mentions it.

Restaurateur Louis Vaudable, whose father became the owner of the restaurant Maxim's in 1932 and who succeeded him in 1942, later claimed to have discovered the secret during a dinner at the Tatin sisters' inn while hunting in Sologne, which is very unlikely since the Tatin sisters died in 1911 and 1917, respectively, when Louis Vaudable, born in August 1902, was not yet 15 years old.

Strawberry Cheesecake

For the base:

- 100 g of biscuits (such as Petit Beurre)
- 80 g of unsalted butter

For the filling:

- 500 g of cream cheese (such as Philadelphia)
- 200 g of granulated sugar
- 4 eggs
- 250 g of strawberries

For the strawberry coulis:

- 250 g of strawberries
- 200 g of granulated sugar
- Juice of 1/2 lemon

Preparation:

Preheat your oven to 180°C.

Crush the biscuits into fine crumbs using a food processor.

Melt the butter and mix it with the biscuit crumbs.

Spread this mixture in the bottom of a springform pan, pressing it down firmly. Chill in the refrigerator.

Wash the strawberries, hull them, and cut them into pieces.

In a large bowl, beat the cream cheese with the sugar and eggs until smooth and homogeneous.

Gently fold the strawberry pieces into the mixture.

Pour this mixture over the biscuit base in the pan.

Bake for 40 minutes at 180°C. Let cool before removing from the pan.

Preparation of the strawberry coulis:

Blend the strawberries with the sugar and lemon juice until smooth.

Strain the coulis if necessary to remove the seeds.

Assembly:

Once the cheesecake has cooled, generously top it with the strawberry coulis.

Chill in the refrigerator for at least 2 hours before serving.

Pear and Chocolate Sponge Cake

Ingredients:

For the sponge cake:

- 4 eggs
- 130 g of granulated sugar
- 130 g of flour
- 1/2 packet of baking powder

For the filling:

- arg can of pears in syrup
- 250 g of dark chocolate
- 4 egg yolks
- 6 egg whites
- 2 tablespoons of liquid fresh cream

Preparation of the sponge cake:

Preheat your oven to 180°C.

Separate the egg whites from the yolks.

Beat the egg whites with a pinch of salt until stiff peaks form. When they are firm, add the sugar and continue beating.

Reduce the speed of the mixer and add the egg yolks all at once, then the flour and baking powder, sifting them in.

Mix quickly so that the batter does not deflate, then pour into a buttered and floured mold.

Bake for about 20 minutes. Let cool before removing from the mold and slicing the sponge cake in half horizontally.

Preparation of the chocolate mousse:

Melt the dark chocolate in a double boiler until smooth.

Off the heat, add the egg yolks one by one, then the fresh cream.

Beat the egg whites until stiff and gently fold them into the chocolate mixture.

Assembly:

Drain the pears in syrup and reserve the juice.

Soak the base of the sponge cake with the pear syrup and a drop of dark rum.

Place a cake ring around the sponge cake to maintain its shape.

Pour half of the chocolate mousse over the sponge cake and smooth the surface.

Cut the pears into slices and arrange them on the sponge cake to cover the entire surface.

Pour the remaining chocolate mousse over the pears and smooth the surface.

Refrigerate for at least 4 hours before serving.

My Little Bonuses Just for You

Essential Kitchen Utensils

Cooking is good, but cooking well is better!

But which utensils should you use? What are the essentials in the kitchen?

I have compiled a list of equipment that you should have to get started. This list is obviously not exhaustive. You can add to it as you progress.

For Measuring:

A Measuring Cup
The measuring cup (like the scale) remains indispensable in the kitchen. Ideally, you should have a Pyrex measuring cup with a handle and lid. The handle will prevent you from burning yourself if the cup is hot when you need to measure a hot liquid. The lid will allow you to store your cup in the fridge without dirtying another utensil.

An Electronic Scale
An indispensable tool, especially for baking, make sure it measures to the gram. You can find affordable ones.

Pour cuire:

Small Saucepans
For preparing sauces or cooking small quantities.

A Medium-Sized Wok
You can even use it for frying.

Pans of Various Sizes

A Medium-Sized Cast Iron Dutch Oven with Lid
For simmering or cooking vegetables. It is indeed an investment, but the results are excellent. It is a good investment as it is a utensil that lasts a lifetime.

A Steamer

A Large Pot or Large Saucepan
For cooking pasta, making mussels marinière, etc…

A Pressure Cooker
Allows for quick steaming of dishes. There are classic models and more sophisticated ones.

For Information

A "**russe**" is another name for a saucepan. However, this term specifically refers to a tin-lined copper saucepan with fairly high straight sides and a rather thin handle. This term is used by professional chefs.

Sauté Pans are saucepans with low sides that gradually flare out, either straight or rounded.

Sautoirs are pans with high, straight sides, a flat bottom, and a long handle.

Rondeaux are similar in shape to sautoirs but have two "ears" (handles) that make them easier to transfer to the oven and serve at the table.

For Cutting, Slicing, and Chopping:

Good knives are essential for proper cooking. Don't hesitate to invest a good budget in them.

A good paring knife

A peeler or a vegetable peeler
For peeling your fruits and vegetables.

A slicer

A utility knife

A fillet knife
Flexible blade for filleting fish.

... and a cutting board

A honing steel
Used to sharpen knives to restore their edge effortlessly.

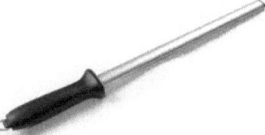

A knife sharpener
You can find manual ones for the more economical option and electric ones for the more sophisticated.

♫ Sharpening and Honing a Knife

- Sharpening is done when the knife is dull, using a diamond or ceramic honing steel, a sharpener, a stone, or a manual sharpener.

- Honing is done daily with a honing steel to maintain the knife's edge.

A mandoline
Not necessarily indispensable, but it can become so as you progress.

A grater

A garlic press
Designed to crush garlic cloves to extract a fine puree. It is easy and effective to use.

A mortar
Accompanied by its pestle, this very practical tool will allow you to grind all your preparations with ease! It is ideal for spices or other ingredients you wish to grind. You can also use it as a container or an ice bowl.

For the Oven... and More!:

Gratin Dishes
For making gratins, lasagnas, etc.

A Baking Sheet (parchment paper is an alternative)

Cake Molds
They are not just for baking; they are very useful in cooking too. Cakes, quiches, or savory muffins, you can make it all!

A Silicone Baking Mat
Preparations adhere to the baking mat without sticking.

For Mixing, Kneading, and Beating:

An Electric Mixer

A Maryse (Silicone Spatula)
Used for scraping and spreading. In silicone, it is also very useful for not damaging pans.

A Whisk

A Mixing Bowl
A stainless steel container that resembles a salad bowl with a rounded bottom. It is used for whisking, stirring, and pouring.

Wooden Spoons
To avoid damaging your cooking utensils.

A Multi-Function Food Processor

Bowls of Various Sizes

Food Storage:
Transparent containers (various sizes).

Others:

A Fine-Mesh Strainer

A Timer

A Can Opener

A Trussing Needle
Accompanied by kitchen twine, it allows you to secure poultry and game optimally for a beautiful presentation and even

cooking. The trussing needle can also be used to check the doneness of the meat.

Cookie Cutters Ideal for decorating, making cookies, vol-au-vents, bites, etc...

A Piping Bag and Decorating Tips

- The piping bag is a conical bag fitted with a tip called a nozzle, used in cooking to decorate or fill dishes.

- The nozzles are usually made of stainless steel or polycarbonate (plastic). There are many types of nozzles, suited to different uses.

- **Plain Nozzles:** Round with various diameters.

- **Star Nozzles:** Round with teeth.

- **Petit-Four Nozzles:** Star nozzles with many fine teeth to create texture.

There is also a wide variety of decorating nozzles, allowing you to create shapes such as roses, leaves, etc.

A Rolling Pin, Spatulas, and a Pastry Brush

The Different Knives Used by Professional Chefs ... and Other Cutting Utensils

KITCHEN KNIVES

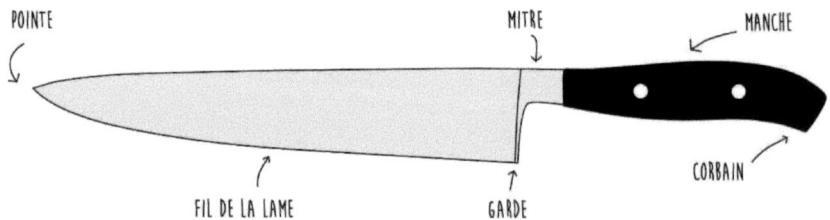

POINTE   MITRE   MANCHE

FIL DE LA LAME   GARDE   CORBAIN

Bird's Beak Knives

The bird's beak knife is a small, very handy knife. The blade of the bird's beak knife is curved inward, making it easier to cut round fruits and vegetables. It also makes peeling potatoes easier.

Foie Gras Knives

Knives with perforated blades are recommended, so that the slice of foie gras can slide cleanly on the cutting surface, saving time and increasing efficiency.

Chef's Knives

You can use a chef's knife to slice, chop, or mince your food:

- Slice your chicken fillets to make strips of the right size, or to make thin slices of beef for your Japanese woks.

- Finely chop your fresh herbs like chives or basil into small, delicate pieces.

- Quickly chop your vegetables into brunoise or julienne for successful dish accompaniments.

Bread Knives
The bread knife is a long (18 to 30 cm) serrated knife that allows you to easily cut all types of bread.

Paring Knives
A paring knife is a small knife with a short, pointed blade,  without serrations. The straight paring knife: Short and rigid blade, it is essential for peeling vegetables, and cutting into cubes or slices.

Fillet Knives or Fish Knives
The fillet knife will be very useful for cutting all types of fish with precision.

Pizza Knives
The pizza knife has a serrated blade that allows for clean and precise cuts. The rounded and high blade provides cutting comfort.

Boning Knives
The boning knife is the butcher's favorite! It efficiently skins and slices tendons and fats. It is ideal for cutting large pieces of bone-in meat, poultry, or any other game... A very characteristic blade: thin and curved to ensure a smooth cut, easily deboning the meat and cutting it.

Slicing Knives
Specially designed for vegetables, the slicing knife has a rigid and

thick blade that allows for chopping and cutting all vegetables into cubes. This professional knife also allows for slicing and cutting.

Chinese Chef's Knives
The Chinese chef's knife is used for its large blade surface and the ease of cutting it provides. It is ideal for chopping fine herbs and vegetables, as well as cutting meats and fruits.

Cheese Knives

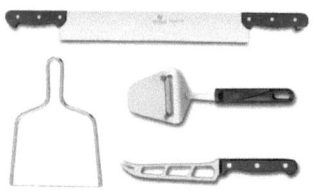

You can find cheese knives with a single handle (for smaller pieces) or double handles, which are perfect for slicing large wheels. The shape of the blades is also designed according to your use, with square and thick blades, or pointed blades to pick up pieces once cut.

Oyster Knives

Ham Knives
Its long, thin, and flexible blade is originally intended for slicing cooked, dried, or smoked ham. However, it can also be used to slice salmon. Be careful with storing your ham knife as the blade length can reach up to 25 cm!

Japanese Santoku Knives
It is the equivalent of the chef's knife. Its particular blade has a curved cutting surface at the tip. When cutting, a rocking motion is automatically created, making the task easier for the cook. This blade can be hollow-ground, creating micro air bubbles between the steel and the cut food, making cutting

even easier. The Santoku knife is one of the essentials for fine and smooth cutting while respecting the food.

Salmon Knives

These kitchen knives with long and flexible blades allow for easy slicing of raw or smoked salmon, as well as slicing ham pieces. The blade is sometimes hollow-ground to reduce adherence to the sliced product. These knives are very durable but especially robust thanks to their all-stainless steel material.

Steak Knives

The steak knife can be used both at the table and in the kitchen. Steak knives are designed to slice steaks and other cooked or raw meats. High-end steak knives have a smooth blade, which allows for slicing rather than tearing the meat. Some also have a micro-serrated blade for easy maintenance.

Sushi Knives

The Japanese sushi knife is a slicing knife (Yanagi) ideal for cutting sashimi and sushi slices. It has a very long and very solid blade, allowing the knife to glide over the fish without pressure. The blade is also very narrow, to stick as little as possible to the fish. The cuts are very clean and precise. Finally, it is often sharpened on only one side (asymmetrical).

Thai Carving Knives

It is a small knife specially designed for carving fruits and vegetables. It can come in several models, such as the stylus (a straight knife with a often flexible blade), or the bird's beak (its rigid blade allows for cutting thick skins).

Tomato Knives

The tomato knife is a small kitchen knife with a serrated blade of 12 to 15 cm in length. This allows for easy slicing of tomatoes.

Slicing Knives
The slicing knife allows you to cut large pieces of meat into thin slices but also for cutting all kinds of fish. Its long and smooth blade allows for slicing in one pass with great comfort.

Utility Knives
The utility knife is a knife with a 10 to 16 cm thick blade. It is used for peeling fruits, chopping vegetables, cutting cheese, and mincing garlic cloves. Like the chef's knife, it is extremely versatile, except when it comes to tackling meat... Its rather short blade makes it a knife halfway between the paring knife and the chef's knife.

Vegetable Knives
These knives have solid blades and tips with a smooth edge. They are mainly designed for cleaning, cutting, and peeling fruits and vegetables. These knives are also made with a bird's beak-shaped blade, most often in stainless steel to provide great resistance to corrosion.

Cleavers and Choppers
The cleaver is a large knife with a wide, flat blade. It is a tool intended for cutting bones and fish bones. It 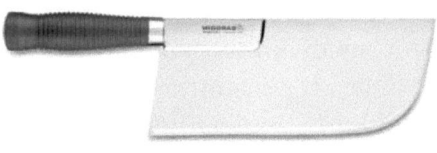 is used on meats, poultry, and crustaceans. Be sure to use a thick cutting board on a stable surface to avoid cutting anything other than the meat.

Butcher Knives
The butcher knife facilitates meat cutting.

Carving Knives
These butcher knives are mainly used for cutting all types of meat, whether ham, poultry, roasts, and others. The handle and blade of these professional knives are designed to facilitate use and performance. They are robust tools with great durability.

Nerve Knives
This professional butcher knife will allow you to easily remove nerves. Some have flexible blades for even more comfortable use.

Skinning Knives
These knives are used to remove the skin from dead animals and are intended for professional chefs and knowledgeable amateurs.

Dessert Knives
Designed to facilitate cake cutting, their long and serrated blades will make your cut in one pass.

Paring Knives
The paring knife is mainly used to thin meats or fish. With a fairly long and flexible blade, it allows you to remove all nerves and fat from the meat.

Bleeding Knives
These knives have a thick and pointed blade that allows for piercing. These knives are intended for butchers and are made with a steel blade.

Sausage Knives

The sausage knife has a serrated blade like the bread knife, making it particularly effective for penetrating the sausage's flesh. These knives are perfect for sausages but also suitable for tomatoes or small bread rolls.

Tripe Knives

These very specific knives are perfect for skinning sheep and other meats, to prepare them in the best way.

Bonus

Ceramic Knives

Ceramic knives are trendy, and it's important to provide some usage tips for those who want to equip themselves.

Ceramic knives are ideal for cutting fruits, vegetables, boneless meats, fish fillets, and charcuterie. Use ceramic knives on a wooden or plastic cutting board.

Never use your ceramic knife for deboning, prying, cutting hard or frozen foods, as you risk breaking the blade. Ceramic is very strong from back to front but remains fragile in torsion from left to right (or vice versa). The hardness of ceramic is higher than that of steel, so if you follow these usage tips, you won't need to sharpen your ceramic knife.

If you use your ceramic knife intensively, there are special sharpeners for ceramic knives.

You will, of course, find low-end ceramic knives for a few euros in supermarkets and other bazaars... If you want to try ceramic, it's better to invest a bit more to get a quality knife.

Carbon Knives
Carbon knives are renowned in the culinary world because they are extremely sharp, and their cutting ability lasts over time. These knives have a higher-than-average carbon content, often around 1%.

What is the advantage of carbon? This element is an important factor in hardness; it will consolidate the blade and make it solid for a long time.

Due to this solidity, the cutting edge is much harder and can withstand more intensive sharpening, but also maintain it over the long term.

That's why carbon kitchen knives are known for their marked and durable cutting ability! The compositions of carbon steel can vary depending on their origin. Carbon knives are also easy to maintain, with a honing steel or sharpening stone: their edge is easily shaped.

Knives with carbon blades are oxidizable and require special care!

They are intended for experienced cooks!

Indeed, they often have little (or no) chrome, which contributes to the stainlessness of the alloy. Thus, they are sensitive to moisture: they must be washed by hand (definitely not in the dishwasher) and dried immediately after washing.

You can also oil them from time to time with mineral oil to protect them. Even if their maintenance is different and more complex than other knives, they are really worth it and will accompany you for years.

Thus, these knives will make you forget about stainless steel knives!

Other Cutting Utensils

Channel Knife
It allows you to make incisions in the skin of your fruits and vegetables, like grooves. This is possible thanks to a small tooth located on the top of the channel knife, which digs into the food. Its small size prevents removing too much material, so as not to damage  the food underneath. The channel knife allows you to decorate fruits and vegetables for beautiful presentations. You can use a channel knife to decorate a lemon, an orange, or even a zucchini or a carrot. You can create lines or curves for an original visual effect.

Kitchen Scissors
You can use your kitchen scissors for cutting poultry, herbs, pies, etc. These utensils are very practical when you want to achieve precision or very small sizes.

Peelers and Parers

A good peeler is essential for small tasks in the kitchen. It allows you to remove the skin from your fruits and vegetables without wasting the flesh.

Mandoline Slicer

This is a cutting tool that allows you to slice foods to varying thicknesses. It provides quick results and is very practical to use! The mandoline allows you to cut your fruits, like apples and pears, as well as your vegetables, evenly. It works on small or large pieces, from radishes to celery, including beets and onions...

Apple Corer

A kitchen tool designed for decoration. Also called a "Parisian apple corer," it allows you to prepare small balls about 2 cm in diameter from your favorite fruits and vegetables.

Apple Corer

It allows you to completely core an apple in one go! The apple corer is a straight tool shaped like a tube. Simply place it on the top of the apple when it is flat and push it into the fruit's flesh. The central part (which contains the core) is cut in one stroke.

Butter Curler

This is a tool that allows you to decorate your dishes! Simply scrape your butter block with the butter curler to form pretty curls. It's perfect if you want to beautifully garnish your buffets or surprise your guests with a professional presentation.

Zester

This is an easy-to-use accessory. Its stainless steel cutting surface has five small teeth, allowing you to easily grate the skin of citrus fruits (lemons, grapefruits, oranges...) to produce a large quantity of zest. The zest will add flavor to all your preparations and can also serve as decoration to brighten up your appetizers, main courses, and desserts.

V-Shaped Melon Knife

Allows you to open melons, squashes, and other large fruits and vegetables while decorating them.

Vegetable Cutter

Allows you to create fun slices for your vegetables, fruits, as well as butter and cheese. You can also make wavy chips with this accessory.

Egg Slicer

The operation is simple: just place the egg under the wires, in the handle's groove, and press the accessory in one motion. The result is clean, quick, and consistent!

Grater

For hard cheeses, carrots, zucchinis, nuts, or even chocolate (to make perfect shavings for decorating your pastries).

Vegetable Spiralizer

It works like a school pencil sharpener. Insert the vegetable to be cut into one of the cylinders (depending on its size) and turn the vegetable on itself. The vegetable's flesh will come into contact with the internal blade and be cut into tagliatelle. It is suitable for carrots, zucchinis, cucumbers... You can incorporate the thin vegetable strips obtained into your woks, pasta, salads...

The Different Traditional Sizes of Vegetables and Fruits

Balled Cutting fruits or vegetables into balls is not complicated, but it always wins a little success at the table. Normal: seeing balls of vegetables or fruits changes from sticks or cubes!

To achieve this aesthetic and fun cut, you just need to have a tool in your drawer: the Parisian scoop, which allows you to scoop out the flesh of vegetables or fruits into small balls.

A little trick: to prevent our vegetable balls from oxidizing too quickly, we can dip them in a bowl of cold water before cooking them.

Bias Cut The bias cut is often used for vegetable preparations in a wok. In fact, as its name does not necessarily indicate, cutting vegetables into bias means cutting them into slices (more or less thin, depending) but obliquely. A fairly original diagonal cut that just requires good consistency in the cut!

Brunoise Brunoise is a vegetable cut that requires a bit more experience and precision! Logically: cutting vegetables into brunoise means cutting pre-washed and peeled vegetables (or fruits) into very small cubes, 2mm thick, no more!

To achieve this, a little trick: first, cut your vegetables into slices of the same size, then cut them into thin sticks horizontally. Only then do you cut them vertically to form small squares!

Chiffonade The so-called chiffonade cut is specific to leafy vegetables like salads, endives, cabbages, or spinach, for example. Why this particularity? Simply because to cut a vegetable into chiffonade, you need to roll its leaves on themselves and cut the vegetable along its entire length!

Julienne Julienne is a cut that once again requires patience and precision! Indeed, to cut vegetables into julienne, you need to wash, peel, and cut them into very thin sticks (5 cm long, 2 mm thick).

This way, you will get a beautiful julienne of vegetables that you can use either as a decorative garnish or in spring rolls or nems, for example. To cut vegetables into julienne, first pass them through a mandoline to get thin slices (2 mm thick), then cut them into sticks!

Macédoine When preparing a homemade vegetable macédoine, we often don't realize it, but we are performing a fairly technical vegetable cut: the macédoine cut. Yes: cutting vegetables into macédoine means cutting them into very small cubes, 3 to 4 mm thick (barely thicker than for a brunoise, in fact). This cut is not only used for the famous macédoine but also for fruit salads or vegetable accompaniments!

Mirepoix Mirepoix is a vegetable cut that is a bit less known to beginners than julienne or brunoise. Well, in theory, because in practice, cutting vegetables into mirepoix means cutting them into small cubes 1 cm thick. Simply!

Paysanne The paysanne cut (or à la paysanne, it works too) is a fairly traditional cut often used for aromatic garnishes or soups. Specifically, it involves cutting vegetables into small squares or small triangles 1 cm thick.

Sliced When you want to make a cucumber salad, a tomato tart, or a zucchini gratin, there is an essential cut you need to master: slicing into fairly thin rounds, also known as slicing!

Unsurprisingly, this is one of the first vegetable cuts you learn in cooking: it just requires a good paring knife, a cutting board, and a minimum of attention to avoid injuries!

Tagliatelle The tagliatelle cut consists of making long and thin ribbons of vegetables. It is, of course, a very visual cut that gives a very professional and well-thought-out look to any vegetable garnish! You can make vegetable tagliatelle with zucchini, carrots, and even radishes! For easier cutting, it is recommended to swap your old peeler for a mandoline: the work will be more precise and less arduous!

Summary

Stick Cuts	
Cut	**Dimensions**
Julienne	1 x 1 x 60 mm
Jardinière	5 x 5 x 50 mm
Matchstick	3 x 3 x 60 mm

Dice Cuts	
Cut	**Dimensions**
Macédoine	5 x 5 x 5 mm
Mirepoix	10 x 10 x 10 mm
Brunoise	2 x 2 x 2 mm

Other Cuts	
Cut	**Dimensions**
Paysanne	Square or triangle shape, 2 mm thick
Ciseler	Finely sliced (less than 1 mm cubes)
Turned	Oval shape
Parisian Scoop	Shaped into balls with a Parisian scoop

Some Other Culinary Terms

A l'anglaise: English-style cooking: cooking vegetables in boiling salted water.

Abaisse: A piece of dough (shortcrust, sweet, etc.) rolled out with a rolling pin to reduce its thickness.

Abaisser: The action of rolling out dough on a floured board to reduce its thickness using a rolling pin or a dough sheeter, so it can be cut with a cookie cutter or used to line a mold. The rolled-out dough is called "abaisse."

Acidify or Acidulate: To make a sauce more acidic or sour by incorporating lemon juice or vinegar.

Adjust: To correct the seasoning and binding of a preparation.

Aerate: To incorporate air into a preparation by sifting, mixing, or whisking.

Appetizer: A dish served at the beginning of the meal.

Aromatics: Plant substances used to flavor dishes. Aromatics come from all parts of plants; from leaves (e.g., coriander) to bulbs (e.g., garlic) to seeds (e.g., cumin) and fruits (e.g., chili).

Aromatize: To introduce spices and aromatic plants into a preparation to flavor it.

Aspic: A cold savory or sweet preparation in which gelatin has been added to set the mixture.

Baste: To pour juice, sauce, or fat over a roast, poultry, or dish during cooking to keep it tender.

Bain-marie: Gentle cooking of food in a saucepan placed in a larger saucepan filled with boiling water and set over low heat. The bain-marie is used to melt chocolate, make egg-based sauces (hollandaise, sabayon), or keep a sauce warm that cannot be reheated or a preparation that cannot go directly on the heat.

Bain-marie (cooking in): A cooking technique for certain preparations that should not be exposed to high temperatures (genoise, scrambled eggs, coddled eggs, crème caramel, etc.).

Bake: To place a dish ready to cook in a preheated oven at the right temperature.

Ballottine: A small galantine made from a part of poultry (chicken or turkey) shaped like a stuffed leg. This preparation is easy to make with a turkey leg, using the skin with the leg attached. Nowadays, the term ballottine is often used for all small round galantines.

Bavaroise: A cold dessert made from custard or fruit puree with added gelatin and whipped cream.

Béarnaise (sauce): An emulsified sauce made from egg yolks, vinegar, shallots, tarragon, chervil, and butter.

Béchamel: A sauce made from flour and whole milk. Its name is said to originate from Marquis Louis de Béchamel (1630-1703), a famous gourmet at the court of Louis XIV.

Bed: A layer placed under food in the presentation or preparation of a dish (bed of salad...).

Beurre blanc: A sauce made from shallots, vinegar, white wine, and butter, a classic accompaniment for fish, shellfish, and crustaceans.

Beurre Maître d'Hôtel: Soft butter mixed with chopped parsley, lemon juice, salt, and pepper. It can be shaped into a log, wrapped, frozen, and sliced as needed.

Beurre manié: Softened butter mixed with an equal amount of flour. Used for thickening already hot sauces. As it melts gradually, the butter prevents the formation of flour lumps.

Beurre meunière: Brown butter to which lemon juice is added.

Bind: The action of thickening a sauce by adding cream, egg, cornstarch, roux...

Binding: An operation that aims to give a sauce or soup more consistency by mixing in a binding agent, such as egg yolk, flour... When a sauce or soup lacks consistency or smoothness, it is necessary to bind it by adding a substance that will thicken it. Some ingredients simply give body to the liquid to be bound (flour, starch, cornstarch, breadcrumbs, rice cream), while others also add a flavorful principle that modifies or improves the taste (cream, egg, butter, blood).

Bisque: A soup made from a crustacean puree.

Blanc:

- The name given to cooked white poultry fillets (chicken breasts, turkey breasts).
- A mixture of a small amount of flour in the cooking water of certain foods. Cooking technique (preparation): A mixture of flour and cold water added to boiling lemon water and strained (passed through a chinois). Used for cooking artichoke bottoms, certain vegetables, and offal to maintain their white appearance and prevent oxidation.

Blind Baking:
- Baking a pie crust without filling. Parchment paper and/or dried beans are added to the pie crust to prevent it from puffing up during baking.
- A cooking method used to preserve or give certain meats, fish, and vegetables a white color. This cooking is done in a vinegar court-bouillon with flour and fat.

Blond: To lightly sauté food until it reaches a blonde color (onion, shallot, flour, vegetable...).

Blot: To remove moisture or excess fat with a cloth after draining the food.

Bouchées à la Reine: A traditional French pastry consisting of an individual vol-au-vent and its filling.

Bouillon: Liquid resulting from cooking vegetables or meats in water. It serves as a base for many preparations, such as sauces, soups, and broths.

Bouquet: The aroma perceived by the sense of smell that a wine exudes – a bundle of parsley, watercress, etc.

Bouquet garni: A tied bundle of thyme, bay leaf, celery stalk, tarragon, leek greens, and other aromatic plants, used to flavor a dish.

Boil in Salted Water: To cook in boiling salted water with coarse salt. Refresh in ice water.

Braise:
- Slow cooking of a vegetable in fat, covered and without adding water.
- To cook food slowly in a covered pot with a small amount of liquid after browning it in hot fat.

Breadcrumbs: Bread dried in the oven and then ground. Used for making breaded or gratin dishes.

Brown sugar: Crystallized brown sugar extracted from sugarcane juice. It is used in sweet and sour preparations like chutneys and in some recipes from northern and southern France.

Brown: To pass meat or vegetables through hot fat to firm and color the surface. To color meat or vegetables (browned potatoes). To expose meat, vegetables, etc., to high heat (flame, brazier) or high temperature (oven) to brown or grill the surface and possibly make it crispy.

Brush: To spread a thin layer of fat, liquid, beaten egg, etc., using a brush.

Caul Fat or Crepine:
- Fatty membrane surrounding the peritoneum of the pig.

- Fatty membrane surrounding the pig's viscera, in the form of a net. It is used in cooking to hold a preparation (pâté, crépinette, paupiettes) and provide moisture during cooking.

Channel: To make incisions with a channel knife around lemons and other citrus fruits for decoration.

Caramel: Sugar melted with a little water and browned over low heat until it colors.

Caramelization: The process of turning sugar into caramel by heating it gently.

Caramelize:
- To coat a savory or sweet ingredient with caramel.
- To make caramel by gently heating sugar. You can also caramelize food to brown it slightly and enhance its flavor.
- To coat the inside of a mold with a layer of caramel.
- To sauté a vegetable or meat in fat and add a little sugar at the end of cooking to caramelize (onions, endives, meats...).

Casserole: A covered dish for presenting food. Pressure cooker.

Cassolette: A small porcelain, cast iron, or copper dish for presenting food.

Chiffonade: Vegetables or salads cut into thin strips.

Chinois: A very fine strainer shaped like a conical hat.

Chop:
- To reduce to small pieces using a knife or electric chopper.
- To cut food into small pieces using a sharp utensil (e.g., knife, chopper).

Chop finely:
- A method of cutting onions, shallots, etc., into small pieces.
- To cut into very thin slices (cabbage, onion).
- To make diagonal incisions on the surface of a fish with a knife.
- To finely chop herbs or vegetables. To make incisions on a fish, etc., to facilitate cooking.

Clarify:
- The action of making a broth clear by removing the fat and/or impurities from the surface. Do this when the broth is cold.
- A process that separates butter from its milk solids. To do this, heat the butter gently or in the microwave, let it rest. The milk solids will settle at the bottom of the container. Simply skim off the butter on the surface. Clarified butter does not burn during cooking and is used to make delicate sauces like hollandaise.
- The action of separating the egg yolk from the white.
- To make a broth, sauce, or syrup clearer by filtering it. You can also clarify butter by slowly heating it for about thirty minutes to skim off the milk solids, leaving only the fat.

Color: To sear food in hot fat (oil, butter, grease...) to give it a golden color.

Concentration (cooking by): Refers to a cooking method where food is seared in fat, on a direct heat source, or in hot liquid to form a crust on the surface, trapping the juices inside. (e.g., roasting, grilling, frying, sautéing...)

Confit: A method of preserving certain meats by cooking and coating them in fat. Commonly done in the southwest and south of France.

Confite:
- To cook and preserve food in its own fat (pork, goose, duck).
- To preserve various fruit or vegetable preparations in oil, alcohol, vinegar, sugar.
- To cook whole fruits slowly and gently in syrup to confit them.

Cord: Sauce arranged around a dish.

Coulis:
- A thick sauce made from blended cooked or raw fruits or vegetables.
- A generic term used to describe a liquid puree. Coulis contain no starch or flour and are simply pureed and strained. Example: meat, game, shellfish, or vegetable and fruit coulis.

Court-bouillon: A flavored broth made of water, vinegar (white wine for fine preparations), salt, pepper, carrots, onions, bouquet garni, in which the dish is poached.

Cover: To put a lid on a container for cooking or a dish in the oven for braising.

Cream: To add cream to a preparation, soup, or sauce. To soften butter with a whisk by heating it slightly to obtain a smooth and shiny butter.

Crépinette: A type of fatty membrane used to wrap food.

Croque au sel: A way of eating raw vegetables dipped in salt (radishes, tomatoes) often accompanied by buttered bread.

Croustade: A crust made of puff pastry or shortcrust pastry that can contain various foods.

Cook in Papillote: To cook food wrapped in aluminum foil or parchment paper.

Cook in Sauce: To cook with a more or less liquid seasoning used to accompany or cook hot or cold dishes.

Core: To remove the central part of certain fruits (apples, pears...).

Covered (cook in): To cook in a container whose opening is covered, usually with a lid. "Uncovered" means to remove the lid.

Crown (arrange in): To garnish the bottom of a dish with food, leaving a space in the middle (crown of rice).

Crush:
- A term most often used for tomatoes. To do this, seed and peel the tomato (blanch it) and cut it into small cubes.
- To pound in a mortar to reduce to small fragments.

Crush a tomato: To cut a previously blanched and seeded tomato into small cubes.

Crumble: To reduce bread, biscuits, or tuna into small pieces.

Cut Out: To cut shapes from rolled-out dough using a cookie cutter.

Dariole: A dessert made from a flan cream cooked in small molds called "darioles." The name dariole also refers to the cylindrical molds in which these pastries are baked.

Debone: To remove the bones from a piece of meat, poultry, or game.

Decant:
- To remove pieces of meat from a sauce and reserve them in another container.
- Decanting clarified butter means removing the milk solids. (See clarify).
- To transfer a liquid to another container after allowing the solid particles to settle at the bottom. Decanting wine.

Deglaze:
- To add a liquid (wine, water, poultry or veal stock...) to the caramelized juices at the bottom of a pan to make a sauce or jus.
- To lightly moisten the bottom of the pan or pot with cooking juice or alcohol after cooking to make jus or a reduction.

Degrease:

- To remove excess fat from a piece of meat.
- To remove the fat that has formed on the surface of a broth, sauce, etc., with a spoon.
- To remove the fat from the bottom of a pan or pot used to brown food or meat before continuing cooking.

Desalt: To remove the preservation salt from food by soaking it in cold water for a varying amount of time.

Destem: To separate the grains of certain fruits (grapes, currants, gooseberries) from the stem.

Devein: To remove the veins from foie gras, for example, or the intestine from shrimp and some other crustaceans (dark fiber present on their back) with a knife.

Dice: To cut fruits or vegetables into small squares.

Dip: To immerse food in a liquid.

Dressing: Preliminary phases of preparing poultry (stretching, flaming, trimming, emptying, trussing) or fish (scaling, trimming, emptying, washing, drying) before cooking.

Dress: To trim, empty, scale, and wash a fish before cooking. Or for poultry, to flame, empty, and truss it for cooking. To prepare poultry or game, i.e., pluck, empty, flame, and clean.

Dry Cooking: A cooking method that uses air or fat to transfer heat, by conduction or convection. This method allows surface sugars to caramelize.

Dry Out: To make choux pastry over very high heat by kneading it with a spoon until it detaches from the container and forms a compact ball. To subject a preparation to heat to evaporate the moisture it contains. To dry any mixture (choux pastry, duchess potatoes, etc.) by working it continuously with a spatula.

Dot: To butter the surface of a preparation to prevent a skin from forming (soup, cream, sauce).

Dough: The action of mixing flour with butter, eggs, or any liquid, often with all the elements together. For example: making shortcrust pastry, brioche, or baba dough.

Dough Sheeter: A machine for rolling out dough.

Dough Piece: A piece of undivided bread dough.

Duxelles:
- Very finely chopped Paris mushrooms, sautéed in butter with chopped shallots.
- A mixture of chopped mushrooms, onions, and shallots. It is used as a stuffing or garnish.

Egg Wash: The egg wash used in pastry to brown raw dough is simply made with well-beaten eggs; sometimes, yolks are diluted with a little cold water.

Emulsion: A uniform mixture of two (or more) immiscible products. Mayonnaise is an emulsion. The emulsion can be temporary, permanent, or semi-permanent.

Emulsify:

- To intimately mix a fat (butter, oil, sauce) with an egg yolk, mustard, or an ingredient that will bind the preparation.
- To mix two liquid ingredients together without obtaining a completely homogeneous mixture. One of the liquids will form microdroplets dispersed throughout the other. To stabilize the mixture, a third ingredient is necessary.

Express: To press a fruit or vegetable to extract its juice.

Five spices: A blend of spices of Chinese origin composed of star anise, nutmeg, cloves, Sichuan pepper, and fennel.

Foam: A mass of light bubbles formed by gases developed or retained in an agitated, heated, or fermented liquid. The substance called sea foam, used to make pipes, is hydrated magnesium silicate.

Flake:
- To break up the cooked flesh of fish or poultry with your fingers.
- To remove the leaves from an aromatic plant.

Flambé:
- To pour heated alcohol over a preparation and ignite it. This reduces the amount of alcohol while modifying the flavors of the dish.
- To quickly pass a piece of poultry or game under a flame to remove the down.

Flank: To arrange a garnish around a central piece.

Fleurons: Small crescent-shaped decorations made from puff pastry to decorate dishes.

Fold: To gently incorporate one mixture into another by folding the preparations over each other from the edge of the container to the center.

Four-Spice: A blend of white pepper, ground cloves, grated nutmeg, and ginger.

Freeze:
- The action of transforming a liquid, cream, or syrup into ice.
- To surround the ice cream maker or mold containing ice cream with crushed ice (4/5) and coarse salt (1/5).

Freezing: To solidify a mixture in an ice cream maker or turbine.

Fricassee: A cooking method in a pot for foods cut into pieces: chicken, rabbit...

Fry:
- A cooking technique that involves immersing food in a bath of oil.
- To cook food by immersing it in fat to give it a golden and crispy surface.

Gel: To transform a liquid into a gel by adding gelatin in sheet or powder form.

Genoise: A sponge cake batter used in many desserts.

Glazing: The name given to several operations to give a shiny appearance to food – Spreading meat, fruit juice, jelly, etc., on the surface of a dish – Covering cakes with flavored or plain fondant, or, failing that, icing sugar diluted in a little water or egg white with or without flavoring.

Meat Glaze:
- Unthickened stocks reduced to the maximum by evaporation.
- To reduce a meat or poultry stock to a texture close to firm jelly.
- A pasty or syrupy substance obtained by the slow reduction of meat, poultry, or fish stocks. It is then used, among other things, to enhance the flavor of sauces.

Glaze:
- To coat a dessert with chocolate glaze.
- To cover a cake with a thin layer of hot jam or fondant.
- To dip in syrup.
- To set in ice.
- To sprinkle a pastry with icing sugar and caramelize it with a naked flame, in the oven, or with a red-hot iron.
- To color the surface of a sauce or cream under a salamander (grill).
- To brush a juice or jelly on a dish to give it shine.
- To cook food with water and butter. White, without coloring, and brown, with coloring. At the end of cooking, the liquid should be completely evaporated, and the vegetable should be coated and shiny. This cooking method is well-suited for young carrots, turnips, and small onions.

- To color the surface of meat cooked in the oven by basting it with its cooking juices.

White Glaze: To cook vegetables with water, butter, salt, and sugar to achieve a shiny surface after cooking.

Gloss: To apply clarified butter, jelly, or a glaze to the surface of a dish with a brush to make it shiny.

Grainy: A term used for jam or caramelized sugar; it refers to the presence of small sugar lumps the size of grains.

Grease: To coat a mold, baking sheet, or dish with butter or oil using a brush.

Gratin: A golden crust that forms on the surface of a preparation.

Gratinate:
- To sprinkle a preparation with cheese or breadcrumbs and then expose it under the grill to brown the surface.
- To cook a preparation in the oven at high heat to make the surface crispy and golden. Gratin is often made with cheese, cream, or breadcrumbs.

Grill:
- To expose food (meat, poultry, fish, vegetable) directly under the oven grill.
- To toast bread in a toaster or under the oven grill.
- To cook food over high heat on a grill or barbecue.

Gut: To remove the entrails of fish, game, or poultry to prepare it for consumption.

Incorporate: To add an ingredient to a preparation (a mixture).

Infuse:
- To steep an aromatic substance in boiling water to flavor it.
- To temporarily add an aromatic to a liquid preparation to impart its flavor.

Jacket Potatoes: Cooking potatoes in their skins. Start in cold salted water.

Jelly: Clarified juice obtained from fruits, meat, or fish that solidifies when cooled due to the way it has been treated.

Knead: To work dough vigorously to give it elasticity and suppleness.

Lard: To insert strips of lard or small pieces into a piece of meat in the direction of the fibers and at equal intervals using a larding needle.

Larding Needle: A kitchen or butcher's tool used to lard pieces of meat.

Lardons: Pieces of lard cut into small sticks or dice.

Leaven: A ball of bread dough containing fresh yeast and left to "develop," then added to bread dough to inoculate it and make sourdough bread or "raised" tart dough.

Lemon: To rub the surface of certain fruits and vegetables with lemon to prevent oxidation when exposed to air or during cooking. Bananas, apples, avocados, artichoke hearts...

Lift:
- To gently remove the fillets from poultry or fish using a knife.
- The action of lifting a fillet from its base; lifting a sole fillet, etc., lifting a hare saddle fillet.
- To let dough relax so it increases in volume. You can also lift pieces of fish, poultry, or meat. The term means cutting pieces intended for consumption.

Line (a mold): To place parchment paper at the bottom and sides of a mold.

Loosen: To make a preparation more fluid by adding a liquid.

Macédoine: A mixture of finely chopped vegetables or fruits. 5x5x5 mm.

Macerate: To soak food in a cold, flavored liquid (alcohol, oil, lemon juice, wine...) for a varying amount of time to flavor or preserve it.

Marinade:
- A liquid with added aromatics in which meat or fish will soak for a few hours.
- If it is intended to be cooked, vinegar, water, vegetables, and aromatics are used. If it is intended to be raw, it consists only of sliced onions, parsley leaves, aromatics, oil, and lemon juice or vinegar. In both cases, white or red wine or alcohol can be added.

Marinate: To let food rest in a marinade so that it absorbs its flavor before cooking.

Mark: To start cooking food by browning it on all sides. Usually before placing it in the oven to finish cooking.

Mask: To cover an element evenly with a layer of cream, sauce, or jelly.

Melt: To liquefy certain ingredients like butter or chocolate with heat. To cook food covered in fat and its own juices.

Meringue: To cover a dessert or tart with meringue and color it in the oven.

Mesclun: A mixture of several varieties of salad.

Mixture: The combination of different ingredients forming the base of a recipe used to make a dish.

Moist Cooking: A cooking method that uses water or steam to transfer heat. This method highlights the natural flavor of the food.

Mold: To place a culinary preparation in a mold, either to cook it (cake, pâté...), to allow it to gel (eggs in jelly, bavarois...), or to improve its presentation after cooking (pilaf rice...).

Mount with Butter: To add small cubes of cold butter to a sauce.

Pack: To transfer from one container to another to remove air bubbles.

Pan: To cook food covered with fat and aromatic garnish.

Panade: A basic dough used to make choux pastry. It consists mainly of water, butter, and flour.

Papillote: To wrap a preparation in aluminum foil or parchment paper for baking. To make a papillote, cut white parchment paper, fold it in half, and oil the outside carefully. Once the item to be cooked is placed inside, seal it hermetically with beaten egg.

Paupiette: A thin slice of meat prepared as a roll and stuffed.

Paysanne: Cutting vegetables or other foods without following a conventional shape.

Pearl: The action of making raw rice translucent by coating it in oil or butter during the cooking of pilaf rice.

Peel: To prepare a fruit or vegetable by removing its skin to keep only the edible part.

Peel an Orange: To prepare an orange by removing the peel and white skin surrounding it. This is easily done by first cutting off the top and bottom of the fruit. Then, cut the remaining peel into vertical strips all around the orange.

Persillade:
- A mixture of oil, vinegar (salt and pepper), and finely chopped parsley, used in a vinaigrette.
- A mixture of garlic and chopped parsley, sometimes mixed with breadcrumbs.
- Finely chopped parsley

Pies: A pie is a dish of meat or vegetables, cooked and served in a pastry shell, or a sweet tart covered with a pastry layer.

Pinch: To color vegetables, bones, poultry, etc., by fire before adding the cooking liquid. To decorate the edge of a tart with a special pinching tool. To grill on the fire or in the oven. To lightly brown meat to give it color. Also refers to the action of scoring the edge of a tart or pâté.

Pipe: To spread dough on a baking sheet. To line a sauté pan, lay food substances on it: to pipe sole fillets. Layer by layer; alternate layers of different products, etc.

Poach:
- To cook food in water or a liquid below boiling point.
- The action of plunging food (eggs, poultry, fish fillets) into water close to boiling point to cook them.
- To cook in a liquid that is simmering without reaching boiling point. For example, poaching an egg by cooking it without its shell in water with a little vinegar to coagulate the white while keeping the yolk runny.

Praline: A filling of sugar, almonds, or hazelnuts, coated in milk chocolate.

Press: To pass a semi-liquid preparation through a chinois. Press firmly with a pestle to extract the maximum amount of juice.

Prick:
- To make multiple small holes in rolled-out dough with a fork to prevent it from puffing up during baking.

- To insert aromatics into food. Often refers to inserting garlic cloves (or pieces) into incisions made in meat. For example, pricking a citrus fruit with cloves.

Pulp: The flesh of a fruit or vegetable.

Puree: A culinary preparation made from cooked or raw and mashed vegetables.

Quarter: A piece resulting from cutting food into four parts (quarter of meat, quarter of tomato, lemon...).

Rare:
- The degree of cooking for blood duck.
- Meat or other dish that is insufficiently cooked.

Re-emulsify: To emulsify a sauce whose elements have separated, using a mixer, for example.

Reduce:
- To concentrate the flavors of a sauce or juice by cooking uncovered for a long time.
- To boil a liquid over high heat and uncovered to reduce its quantity and intensify its flavor.
- To allow the thickening and concentration of the juices of a liquid preparation to obtain a more intense flavor. This is achieved by leaving the preparation on the heat to reduce its volume by evaporation.

Reduce Cooking: To add cold water to cooking sugar or jam to lower the cooking degree.

Reduction: A composition that has been reduced. (e.g., shallot reduction, reduction for béarnaise...).

Reduce to Glaze:
- To reduce sauces to a glaze.
- To reduce a sauce until it becomes syrupy.

Remove the Rind: To remove the rind from white ham, raw ham, or the rind from salted or smoked bacon.

Reserve: During a recipe, to set aside a preparation or food to use later.

Ribbon (make or form a): A mixture forms a "ribbon" when it becomes thick, and when lifting the spatula or whisk above the utensil, it falls back into the mixture in a ribbon-like stream, slowly sinking back into the mass.

Roast:
- To place spices or nuts (pine nuts) in a hot, dry pan to enhance their flavor.
- To grill foods (coffee, cocoa, nuts) to brown the surface and develop certain aromas.

Roll Out: To lengthen dough using a dough sheeter to achieve the desired thickness.

Roux: A mixture of equal parts softened butter and flour, like beurre manié. However, roux is made by melting butter in a saucepan and then adding flour. The liquid to be thickened is added afterward.

Rub (with garlic): To rub peeled garlic vigorously on a container or croutons.

Sabayon:
- A very light savory or sweet sauce made from egg yolks, cooked in a bain-marie while incorporating a liquid (alcohol, broth).
- A dessert made from a flavored and alcoholic cream made from sugar and egg yolks. Its light and frothy texture is achieved by whisking the cream while heating it in a bain-marie.

Sable: The action of working flour and butter with fingertips to make shortcrust pastry.

Sauté: To fry food in a little fat to firm it up and give it color.

Sauté:
- To quickly brown small pieces of meat, fish, or vegetables in fat.
- To cook food in hot fat while stirring to prevent sticking.
- Food cooked in fat in a special pan with low sides, called a sauté pan or sautoir. Sear the piece on both sides, salt, and remove, then deglaze the pan with water, wine, or cooking stock.

Salamander: A radiant ceiling appliance emitting intense heat, used for glazing, gratinating, reheating, browning, caramelizing, or quickly cooking.

Salpicon: Vegetables, fruits, fish, or meat cut into small dice (between brunoise and macédoine).

Sauce: To coat a preparation with its accompanying sauce.

Scald: To plunge an animal (or vegetable) into boiling water for a few minutes to easily remove the skin.

Scale: To remove the scales from fish with a knife with vertical blades (scaler).

Scrape: To clean the edge of a container thoroughly using a scraper (a flexible rounded plastic sheet), a metal spatula, or a Maryse (a flexible rubber spatula).

Scraper: A small flexible plastic rectangle used to scrape the bottom of containers when transferring to another dish.

Sear:
- To brown meat over high heat to quickly coagulate it.
- To start cooking food by exposing it to high heat to cook the surface while leaving the center raw.

Seed: To remove the seeds from a fruit or vegetable.

Set: To solidify fatty or gelatinous liquids under the action of cold.

Shape: The action of giving a shape to dough or a preparation. Example: shaping small rolls.

Shaker: A bar utensil consisting of two cups and sometimes a filter. It is used to prepare cocktails by vigorously shaking the liquid mixture. It is important to note that a shaker should never be used with carbonated drinks.

Shred: To break up a crumbly food into fine filaments with your fingers or a fork.

Sieve: A kitchen utensil consisting of a very fine mesh, usually metal, used to filter and refine the texture of food.

Sift:
- To pass an ingredient through a strainer to eliminate lumps (sauce, flour...).
- To pass food or a preparation through a sieve to obtain a finer texture free of impurities.

Skewer: To thread a large piece of poultry or meat onto a cooking spit.

Slice:
- To cut almonds and dried fruits into thin slices.
- To remove the "strings" from green beans.
- To remove the intestine from poultry without removing the other viscera.

Smoke Point: The temperature at which fats begin to decompose and smoke.

Smooth:
- To spread the surface of a dessert or cream with a spatula.
- To beat a sauce or cream vigorously with a whisk to make it smooth.

Soak:
- To soak savarins or babas in syrup.

- To rehydrate dried vegetables by placing them in a container with cold water 24 hours before use.

Soften:
- To reduce the acidity or bitterness of a preparation by adding water, cream, sugar, or milk.
- To "blandify" a preparation, giving it a more tolerable flavor by reducing a strong aroma or seasoning (e.g., adding sugar to tomatoes, cream to a soup) or adding sugar to a preparation (see sweeten).

Softened butter: Butter brought to room temperature until it becomes soft and can be worked into a paste.

Spice: To add spices to a dish.

Stale: To let food (usually bread) dry out for a while before consuming it.

Steak: A thick slice cut transversely from a large fish (hake, salmon, tuna).

Stem: To remove the stems from fruits after washing and draining them.

Stew:
- To meticulously prepare a dish.
- To boil a dish slowly and gently in its juice for a long time.

Stiffen: To pass food through hot fat without coloring it. To dip food in hot fat to sear it, either in deep frying or in a pan.

Soak: To wet to allow a liquid (syrup, alcohol, liqueur, milk...) to penetrate various preparations to add moisture and flavor (e.g., soaking a genoise with rum).

Spatula: A kitchen utensil with a long handle and a wide, flat end used to lift food in a pan or to glaze a cake.

Sprinkle: To scatter evenly.

Steam (cooking): A cooking method where heat is transferred to food by contact with steam.

Stock:
- The cooking liquid from braised meat or poultry with seasonings and water. White stock: veal or poultry. Brown stock: beef or game.
- A type of flavored (but unsalted) broth made from meats and vegetables cooked in water for a long time. It is used for sauces, stews, and braises.

Strain: To filter a liquid through a sieve, chinois, or etamine.

Stuffing: A preparation made from chopped foods (meats, vegetables), seasoned and sometimes bound with an egg, used to fill the inside of a fruit, vegetable, meat, or fish.

Summit: The flowering tip of certain plants (in cooking, aromatic plants).

Supreme: The fleshy part of a poultry wing, commonly called "chicken breast."

Stud:

- To stick cloves into an onion. Ideally, leave the onion skin on, which will add a lot of color to the dish.
- To stick pieces of truffle or cloves into a piece of meat or game.

Sweat: To cook food in fat over low heat without coloring. **Sweat (make):** To cook a vegetable in fat over low heat to avoid coloring while losing some or all of its water.

Sweeten: To add sugar, syrup, or a sweetening product to a preparation.

Syrup: The action of coating with syrup; soaking with syrup. Syrup a cake.

Temper: To bring a cooked preparation or a product from the refrigerator (cheese, egg...) to room temperature.

Temper Chocolate: To gently heat chocolate to stabilize it, making it smooth and shiny.

Thicken: To make a liquid preparation thicker by adding a thickening agent (flour, starch...).

Thickener: A substance that thickens a sauce or liquid. Flour and butter, arrowroot, gelatin, and thickeners are thickeners.

Tie: To tie vegetables, a piece of meat, fish, or poultry with string to make cooking more uniform or to hold foods together while they cook.

Tighten:

- The action of beating egg whites very vigorously to make them very firm.
- To reduce a sauce to thicken it.

Toast: A slice of bread, toasted or not...

Toss: An old culinary term; to toss a salad: to turn it over for a long time so that it absorbs the dressing well. Today, we say to mix the salad.

Trimmings:
- Waste or parts that spoil the presentation.
- Skins, nerves, fat removed from meats used to make stocks.

Truffle: To place truffle slices between the flesh and skin of poultry.

Turban: A presentation style for certain dishes in a ring shape.

Turn:
- The action of shaping certain vegetables to improve presentation (small purple artichoke).
- To give a round or regular shape by peeling a food substance.

Untruss: To remove the strings that hold poultry after cooking.

Unmold: To remove a preparation from its cooking mold before serving.

Vanilla caviar: Seeds contained inside a vanilla pod.

Velouté:
- noun: White stock or fish fumet, thickened with a white or blond roux.
- adj.: Refers to a sauce or cream with a certain consistency on the tongue.

Vol-au-vent: A hot appetizer consisting of a round puff pastry shell, usually filled with a garnish called "à la financière."

Well: A well made with flour to add all the necessary ingredients for the recipe in the center and used to form the dough.

Whip: To beat a preparation vigorously to incorporate air (egg whites) or to emulsify a fat (mayonnaise, hollandaise).

Whip to Stiff Peaks: To beat egg whites with a whisk to obtain a foamy preparation of varying firmness and white color by gradually introducing air bubbles.

Wrap: To cover a dish or food with plastic wrap to protect it before placing it in the refrigerator.

Wrap in Caul Fat: To wrap poultry or game in pig caul fat.

Yeast: A substance that transforms the sugars in the food it is incorporated into carbon dioxide, increasing the dough's volume. Yeast can be chemical (also called Alsatian yeast) or biological (fresh yeast, baker's yeast). You can also increase the volume of a preparation mechanically: by incorporating air into egg whites or fresh cream using a whisk inside, seal it hermetically with beaten egg.

Thank you

I would like to express my deep gratitude for your unwavering support.

Thank you for accompanying me to the last page of this book, and especially, thank you for these six years of loyalty and encouragement.

Your enthusiasm for my cuisine has been a constant source of motivation and joy.

It is with passion and dedication that I will continue to explore new flavors and create recipes that will delight your taste buds.

Your trust and support are the heart of my inspiration.

With all my gratitude,

Pascal